Congress, the President, and the Federal Reserve

Congress, the President, and the Federal Reserve

The Politics of
American Monetary Policy-Making

Irwin L. Morris

Ann Arbor

THE UNIVERSITY OF MICHIGAN PRESS

Copyright © by the University of Michigan 2000
All rights reserved
Published in the United States of America by
The University of Michigan Press
Manufactured in the United States of America
⊚ Printed on acid-free paper

2003   2002   2001   2000   4   3   2   1

A CIP catalog record for this book is available from the British Library.

Library of Congress Cataloging-in-Publication Data

Morris, Irwin L. (Irwin Lester), 1967–
    Congress, the president, and the Federal Reserve : the politics of
American monetary policy-making / Irwin L. Morris.
        p.   cm.
    Includes bibliographical references and index.
    ISBN 0-472-10995-2 (alk. paper)
    1. Monetary policy—United States.   2. Board of Governors of the
Federal Reserve System (U.S.)   I. Title.
HG540.M67   1999
332.4'973—dc21   99-015912

For Chris and Maddie

Contents

Acknowledgments

This book—like others, I suppose—is both a solitary and a communal endeavor. It is the product of long and often lonely hours spent in libraries, computer labs, and offices. It is also, in an important way, the product of the criticisms and suggestions of a number of intelligent colleagues and friends. In the end, I take responsibility for all of the errors contained herein; however, I cannot take full credit for whatever is of quality.

First, I thank the members of my dissertation committee. In particular, I am indebted to my chair, Bill Keech, and committee member Mike Munger. Both gave extensive and invaluable assistance in the preparation of my dissertation—the first draft of this book. Bill Bernhard, Craig Emmert, and Trey Hood provided useful comments on various versions of portions of the manuscript, and I am in their debt. I am grateful to the graduate school at the University of North Carolina for both indirect (a graduate fellowship) and direct (a dissertation fellowship) support of this project. I am also grateful to Chuck Myers, Kevin Rennells, and other members of the editorial staff at the University of Michigan Press who contributed to the quality of this book. Likewise, I appreciate the many insightful comments of two anonymous reviewers.

Finally, I thank my wife, Chris. If it were not for her support and her patience during too many lonely days and nights, I could not have finished this project.

CHAPTER 1

Introduction

> The Federal Reserve System is perhaps the most controversial non-elected element of the government of the United States. Journalists and voters vilify it, Congress and the President seek to dominate it, and scholars argue about it. (Munger and Roberts 1990, 83)

Among federal bureaucracies, the Federal Reserve (or Fed) is at least first among equals. Though it is neither the oldest nor the largest federal agency, it has a greater impact on the course of everyday economic life than does any other bureaucracy or regulatory agency. Although the Fed has a number of important duties—acting as a clearinghouse for commercial banks, regulating certain banking activities, and printing and issuing currency—the Fed's most important responsibility is the conduct of monetary policy (the manipulation of the quantity of money in circulation). This responsibility also provides the Fed with the power to influence the national and international economy. As Newton wrote, "In America one institution, more than any other, controls the movement of money, prices, and the economy. That institution is America's central bank, the Federal Reserve" (1983, 10). In reality, "No one can afford to ignore the Fed" (Beckner 1997, ix).

That such a powerful institution would be a political animal in a political jungle seems obvious. But the politics of monetary policy-making were long ignored by students of the Fed, and only during the past 30 years—much less than half the Fed's life—have the political dimensions of Fed policy-making served as a focal point for research. During this time, scholars have suggested and developed a number of different perspectives toward the politics of monetary policy-making, and this multiplicity of theoretical viewpoints has led to a wide array of empirical analyses designed to evaluate the claims of various theories.

At the beginning of the research that would eventually lead to this book, I fully intended to conduct what would be—at least for a time—the definitive empirical evaluation of extant theories of Fed policy-making. As a graduate student in political science, I understood that work of that type was the substance of many a "good" dissertation. I also knew, though only half-consciously at the start, that making an original theoretical contribution was a far more difficult endeavor. During the months in which I submerged myself in the monetary policy-making literature, I became convinced that my intentions were misguided. I no longer believed that any type or quantity of empirical analysis would resolve the controversies over the politics of Fed policy-making. I came to realize that traditional perspectives toward monetary policy simply failed to offer an adequate characterization of politics at the Fed. And so I delved into another literature—the formal literature on regulatory policy-making—in an effort to understand the Fed. This book is the result of my efforts to use that literature to develop a new theory of the politics of monetary policy.

From an institutional perspective, the Fed is a peculiar creature. It is privately owned but publicly controlled. Private citizens own the stock of the 12 Federal Reserve Banks (Atlanta, Boston, Chicago, Cleveland, Dallas, Kansas City, Minneapolis, New York, Philadelphia, Richmond, St. Louis, and San Francisco), and the individual Federal Reserve Banks are responsible for lending to private banks and conducting the necessary clearinghouse processes for these private institutions. The "command post" of the Federal Reserve System is, however, in Washington, where the Federal Open Market Committee and the Board of Governors meet.

The Federal Open Market Committee (FOMC), like the System itself, has an unusual public/private character. The FOMC, responsible for guiding the Open Market Desk's sale and purchase of government securities (a monetary policy known as open market operations) is composed of the seven members of the Board of Governors and five of the regional reserve bank presidents. The FOMC determines the target rate for the Federal Funds interest rate (Fed Funds rate). The Fed Funds rate is the rate at which commercial banks make overnight loans to other commercial banks, and it is an important indicator of the cost and availability of short-term liquidity. The reserve bank presidents represent the private component of the FOMC. The presidents are chosen by the shareholders of the institutions that they represent, though their selection is subject to the advice and consent of the Board of Governors. The members of the Board of Governors represent the public side of the FOMC. They are appointed by the president and confirmed by the Senate. They serve 14-year terms, the longest of any federal official except the director of the General Accounting Office and federal court justices. The predominance of the public component of the FOMC is reflected in the fact that only five of the twelve reserve bank presidents have voting rights on the FOMC at any point in time.[1] Therefore, the governors always enjoy a seven to five, public versus private, majority.

Another peculiar Fed trait, at least as far as federal agencies are concerned, is the manner in which it generates revenue for operating costs and other expenditures. The Fed does not make formal budgetary requests of Congress, and Congress does not make appropriations from the public coffers to fund Fed expenses. So how does the Fed raise the money to pay for its expenses? It owns a large portfolio of government securities on which it receives interest payments, and the Fed's securities transactions (i.e., the sale of government securities through open-market operations) also generate revenue for the System. Likewise, the Fed collects fees from private banks for certain banking services. Even in the absence of congressional appropriations, the Fed has no "budget" problems. In fact, the Fed gives billions of dollars in excess revenue to the Treasury Department every fiscal year—largesse from the bounty of its earnings. Thus, the Fed is a completely self-funding organization, a characteristic that makes it unique among federal agencies. So in important ways, the Fed is unlike any other federal agency. As Kettl notes,

> The Fed thus occupies a unique place in American government: a public board supervising quasi-private reserve banks, a board free from congressional appropriations and Presidential oversight, a board composed of officials exercising Congress's monetary powers yet possessing great autonomy and broad flexibility. (1986, 4)

According to one of the Fed's most virulent opponents, Wright Patman, former chair of the House Banking Committee, "A slight acquaintance with American constitutional theory and practice demonstrates that . . . the Federal Reserve is a pretty queer duck" (Greider 1987, 49–50). In short, it is widely considered the most politically independent federal agency.

Given the singular nature of the Fed's power and character, the considerable attention it has generated, both scholarly and otherwise, is no surprise. For all practical purposes, scholars have taken an interest in the Fed and its policy-making activity since its creation. At least two books, Barron's *The Federal Reserve Act: A Discussion of the Principles and Operations of the New Banking Act* and Conway and Patterson's *The Operation of the New Bank Act,* were published about the Fed—or, more specifically, about the Federal Reserve Act—in 1914, the year after its passage. In the intervening 85 years, students of macroeconomics and monetary policy—along with a host of journalists—have published hundreds, if not thousands, of articles and books on policy-making at the Fed.

While research on the Fed has always had an economic or financial component, it has not always included a political component. This is not to say that Fed policy-making was ever apolitical. Any time an institution has the power to influence the quantity of money within circulation—one of the Fed's most important responsibilities—then that institution can potentially affect the character and condition of the economic lives of an entire citizenry. As long as different policy choices generate outcomes that are differentially preferred and these outcomes occur in a policy area that the public considers significant, then policy choices have political implications. Although Fed policy-making has always been political, students of the Fed were not always sensitive to this fact. Because of the institution's ostensible independence, the politics of monetary policy-making were trivialized—or completely ignored—for decades.

Most early studies of monetary policy-making were founded on the assumption that the Fed was a nonpolitical, social welfare–maximizing bureaucracy. The preeminent conceptualization of Fed policy activity was the "public-interest model" (Toma 1991, 157). Explanations of monetary policy were based on dual assumptions: (1) that some socially optimal policy existed and (2) that the Fed attempted to implement that policy. Havrilesky echoes these themes by noting, "During the 1960s monetary policymakers were typically envisioned as idealistically choosing a *socially consensual* 'best' point on a stable, negatively-sloped Phillips Curve" (1995, 11, emphasis added). When the Fed neglected the "proper" course for monetary policy, failure was attributed to the crudeness of the policy tools and the poor quality of the information available to the Fed rather than to potentially undemocratic political machinations. In fact, "Much of macroeconomic policy analysis has been directed toward providing the Fed decision-maker with more refined tools for conducting stabilization policy" (Toma 1991, 158). So it has not always been obvious to scholars that Fed policy-making has a decidedly political dimension.

This is not to say that bankers, politicians, and Fed policymakers failed to recognize the political component of monetary policy: they recognized it from the beginning. The realization that monetary policy was intrinsically political guided the debate over the original proposal to establish the Federal Reserve System, and many economists, bankers, and politicians of the time feared a politically oriented or politically controlled Fed (Kettl 1986; Timberlake 1993; Woolley 1984). J. Lawrence Laughlin, a prominent economist, expressed a common sentiment of the time when he wrote, "We must establish some [banking] institution wholly free from politics or outside influence—as much respected for character and integrity as the Supreme Court" (quoted in Timberlake 1993, 214). Clearly, those present at the Fed's creation realized the potential for political manipulation of the value of money through the central bank's lending practices. However, it seems that most proponents of the Federal Reserve System believed they had achieved the goal, specified by Laughlin, of creating an apolitical or a politically independent institution. In retrospect, however, it is not clear that they were correct in choosing that goal or successful in its attainment. As Timberlake neatly puts it, "They did not know what they had done" (1993, 234). This thinking does, nonetheless, explain why so little attention was paid to the politics of Fed policy-making prior to the late 1960s and early 1970s. If an institution is supposedly apolitical, it hardly makes sense to spend time and energy worrying about the political character of the institution or its policies.

The early dominance of the public-interest perspective also provides an explanation for the scarcity of Fed research conducted by political scientists before 1970. Prior to this time, only a handful of the mass of articles and books on Fed policy-making were written by political scientists (see Woolley 1984, 1994 for a description of this early research). The advent of public-choice theory in the 1960s and 1970s, however, provided the impetus for a reexamination of the public-interest view of monetary policy-making (Toma 1991). The development of public-choice theory revitalized the dormant concern with the politics of monetary policy. One of the basic components of public-choice theory is the assumption that political actors are personal utility maximizers. Given that assumption, there is no obvious reason to assume that a societal goal such as macroeconomic stabilization will result from the activities of political actors. As personnel of a wealthy and powerful federal bureaucracy, Fed policymakers were, by definition, political actors. Likewise, after decades of explicitly apolitical research, students of the Fed became cognizant of the personal political benefits that would accrue to elected politicians if they could control the Fed. Munger and Roberts underscore the political significance of the Fed's responsibilities:

> Because of the importance of the Fed in shaping monetary and overall economic policy, it is a powerful weapon. If political actors could gain control of it and learn how to use it effectively, there is little question that the executive, the Congress, and the other external actors could better their own lot by providing useful service to grateful constituents. (1990, 83)

Over the past 20 years, the study of the politics of monetary policy-making has become increasingly popular. Without exaggeration one can say that scholars have written hundreds of articles and books on the subject,[2] and nearly all of this research focuses on the following general questions: First, what does the Fed do and why? And, given the answer to the first, should the design of institutions for making monetary policy be changed, and if so, how? (Alt 1991).

During the period when the public-interest model dominated thinking about the Fed, attempts to answer the first question dealt with issues of economic information (i.e., What can the Fed know about the character of the macroeconomy?) and economic understanding (i.e., What can the Fed know about the workings of the macroeconomy?). Thus, to understand what the Fed was doing and why it was doing it, one needed to determine what information was available to the Fed and what the Fed took to be the nature of the workings of the macroeconomy. Answers to the question of how to change institutions focused on changing the institutional structure of the Fed so that it might process greater amounts of information more efficiently and develop a more sophisticated and more accurate understanding of the macroeconomy. The political dimensions of Fed decisions did not figure into responses to either question.

The realization that monetary policy included a political dimension generated a reorientation in scholarly attempts to address these important questions. Answers were no longer solely a function of economic factors or issues (i.e., information and understanding): political relationships and political objectives were also viewed as important. Students of the Fed then openly considered the possibility that certain decisions were made for political rather than purely economic reasons. This possibility led to efforts to understand the political dimension of monetary policy and to address questions concerning the political objectives of the Fed and of those actors who might influence Fed policy-making: elected officials such as the president and members of Congress.

The realization that elected officials might influence or manipulate the Fed led to a consideration of the proper role for the president and legislators. The Fed's original architects viewed a significant role for elected officials in monetary policy-making in a very negative light. Not surprisingly, much of the debate concerning the structure of the Fed focused on optimal means of insulating the Fed from political manipulation (see Woolley 1984; Timberlake 1993). But this discussion occurred prior to the Keynesian revolution, which suggested that government—and, implicitly, elected officials—should actively manage the national economy. Thus, cognizance of monetary policy-making's political dimension did not necessarily imply that elected officials could not have a positive impact on the character of Fed policy.[3]

Of course, to determine the roles elected officials should play in monetary policy-making, one must first understand the roles that they do play. How, for example, would monetary policy change if a tight-money president replaced an expansion-minded chief executive? Would the specific impact of this regime change depend on the distribution of policy preferences within Congress? How would a change in party control of the House (or Senate) influence policy? Once these questions are answered, it is possible to evaluate the extent to which institutional changes are likely to aid or hinder the achievement of the policy goals deemed most preferable. Basically, without knowing elected officials' actual effects on monetary policy, it is impossible to draw reasonable conclusions about their proper role in the policy-making process. Effective policy reform requires a sophisticated understanding of the current nature of policy-making. One must understand the inner workings of the policy arena before prescribing change.

The juxtaposition of the immense scope of the Fed's power and influence and the undemocratic character of its formal institutional structure piqued my interest in monetary policy. I began to ask the same questions students of the Fed have been asking for at least a couple of decades: Why is the Fed's institutional structure the way it is? To what extent is the Fed independent of political influence in the guise of presidential or congressional manipulation? If the Fed is not independent of the influence of elected officials, how do these officials implement or exercise their influence or manipulative powers? If the Fed is half as powerful as many journalistic and scholarly accounts contend, then attempting to understand its place (both actual and proper) in the American polity is an important endeavor, because doing so deals with the core issue of a people's capacity to govern themselves effectively.

Students of monetary policy-making have attempted to answer these questions from a variety of different viewpoints. Woolley (1994) argues that the study of the Fed may be divided into at least three schools of thought: the central bank independence (CBI) perspective, the pressure-groups perspective, and the principal-agent perspective. Proponents of the CBI perspective focus on the formal institutional relationship between central banks and their political environments. Politicians are assumed to want inflationary monetary policies; to the extent that central banks—who are assumed to prefer monetary policies that are consistent with price stability—are protected from the pressures and manipulation of elected officials, the banks will act to preserve price stability. Comparative analyses of this type suggest that the Fed is one of the most independent central banks and that political influence plays a relatively minor role in the determination of U.S. monetary policy.

Supporters of the pressure-groups perspective take an opposite tack, suggesting that formal institutions are less important than the informal relationships between policymakers and special interests. Studies within the pressure-group camp focus on the relationship between changes in the policy preferences of important actors in the Fed's political environment (i.e., the president and Congress) and the corresponding changes in monetary policy. Implicitly, the pressure-group perspective is based on the assumption that constellations of political groups make policy. Institutional relationships, while somewhat interesting, are not the core determinant of monetary policy activity.

Principal-agent analyses attempt to combine some aspects of the CBI perspective with a simplified characterization of the Fed's political environment. Usually taking the president or Congress as the principal and the Fed as the agent, principal-agent treatments of monetary policy-making focus on either

1. the Fed's use of its informational advantage to achieve its own policy goals at the expense of those of the president, or
2. Congress or the president's ability to modify the institutional structure of the Fed so that it will be sensitive to either congressional or presidential directives or pressures.

Thus, the findings associated with this perspective are inconsistent, reflecting a schism within the theoretical framework itself.

Given the existence of these various theories it is no surprise that scholars disagree about the answers to the most basic questions concerning the politics of monetary policy. Even in areas of Fed research that have generated the most interest, widely accepted conclusions are the exception rather than the rule. Consider the following questions:

1. Does the president influence Fed policy-making?
2. If presidents do influence Fed policy-making, how do they do so?

Since the early 1970s, a great deal of the research on the political dimension of monetary policy has focused on the relationship between the president and the Fed. No topic in the study of the politics of Fed policy-making has generated more interest than the president's role in the determination of policy. Given the concentration on this particular research area, answers should be found here if they exist anywhere.

Most of the literature on Fed–president relations suggests that the president's policy preferences influence Fed behavior. In fact, some students of monetary politics view the president as the dominant political actor in the monetary policy-making arena (see, e.g., Havrilesky 1988; Hibbs 1977, 1987; Weintraub 1978). Weintraub argues, "What the administration wants or is perceived to want continues to dominate the Federal

Reserve's conduct" (1978, 357). Concurring with Weintraub, Hibbs contends, "monetary policy is quite responsive to the political climate, especially as represented by the preferences of the President" (1987, 8).

Another literature, however, questions the relationship between presidential policy preferences—always difficult to measure accurately—and monetary policy. While Grier (1991) finds evidence of a relationship between the policy preferences of the leadership of the Senate Banking Committee and monetary policy, he finds no evidence of a relationship between presidential policy preferences and Fed policymaking. Likewise, Beck's (1982, 1983, 1987) work casts doubt on the existence of a relationship between presidential policy preferences and monetary policy.

A thorough examination of the relevant literature would likely result in agreement with Woolley's (1994) response to the question of whether the president plays an important role in monetary policy-making:

> We are safe with whatever answer we give, since there is ample evidence that can be introduced to support a negative or a positive conclusion on Presidential influence. However, my own reading of the evidence is unchanged and is in the negative. No, Presidents do not get what they want, but they are *usually* not *very* unhappy with the policy they get. (1994, 75–76)

Thus, the recent conclusion of the one of the most prominent students of monetary policy-making on the issue of presidential influence comes down, technically, on the side of Fed independence. Nevertheless, if "we are safe with whatever answer we give," two decades of research has failed to clear up this fundamentally important aspect of the politics of Fed policy-making.

Likewise, there is as yet no convincing and widely accepted description and explanation of the means by which presidents manipulate or influence monetary policy if they indeed do so. By no means is there a dearth of potential mechanisms for the transmission of influence. Scholars have suggested a variety of means by which presidents might achieve their monetary policy goals. The suggested mechanisms include

1. the power to appoint the chairperson
2. the power to appoint the other members of the Board of Governors
3. presidential signaling through the media
4. the bully pulpit
5. the president's role as legislative leader, and

6. the president's personal powers of persuasion (see esp. Canterbury 1967; Chappell, Havrilesky, and McGregor 1990, 1993, 1995; Havrilesky 1995; Havrilesky and Gildea 1990, 1991, 1992; Kane 1982, 1988; Kettl 1986; Woolley 1984; Yohe 1966).

Nevertheless, a clear exposition of the regular use of any of these tools of influence has never been provided, and other research focuses explicitly on the obstacles associated with the use of one or more of these mechanisms of influence (see Alt 1991 on signaling; Keech and Morris 1997 on appointment power).

Taking a brief look at the literature on the president's role in monetary policy-making—both whether presidents' preferences matter and if so, how do presidents exercise influence—leads to the question of whether scholarship has yet to move beyond preliminary findings and doubtful conclusions. Why are there no answers? The literature's response to this question is empirically oriented: the hypotheses and implications of the various theories have yet to be sufficiently tested and examined. The assumption is that proper testing of the various hypotheses will determine the relative validity of the extant theories and that one of these theories will surely provide the answers.

Not surprisingly, given this theoretical eclecticism, evaluations of the relative quality of each of the theories are based on the empirical record or, more accurately, on scholarly interpretations of the empirical record. Unfortunately, this orientation toward hypothesis testing and theory evaluation has resulted in the false hope that one theory might receive the overwhelming preponderance of empirical support. What should be clear now, and quite possibly should have been clear long ago, is that a definitive resolution—based on extant theories—is unlikely to occur.

Responses to this problem—once it is recognized—can take two not necessarily mutually exclusive forms: scholars can (1) gather greater amounts of higher-quality data and analyze the data with increasingly sophisticated methodologies in the hopes that one perspective will win greater support and the others will be discredited, and/or (2) reformulate the theoretical structure of the field. The first option implies that the explanatory failure of the literature is a data or methodological problem. Thus, if there were data of sufficient quality (i.e., valid and reliable measures of the president's monetary policy preferences) and adequate methodological tools, the inconsistencies in the empirical record would disappear and one of the extant theories would rise above the fray as the winner. The second option implies that extant theories cannot provide an adequate explanation of the phenomena of concern. In this case, no increase in the quality or amount of data or the sophistication of analytical techniques will solve the problem, as data and methods are only as good as the theories tested.

I do not mean to say that one cannot move on the theoretical and empirical fronts at the same time. I, in fact, attempt to do so here. I do, however, want to emphasize shortcomings associated with choosing the first of the two options. This discussion is specifically intended to highlight the problems associated with attempting to solve what is an intrinsically theoretical problem by throwing data and methods at it.

In some areas of research, seeking out new explanations for empirical phenomena is a common endeavor. These areas tend to be those in which there is either no extant explanatory theory appropriate for the phenomena or those in which a single extant theory is viewed as no longer being up to the task of organizing and explaining the relevant components of the empirical world. In cases such as these, the development and elucidation of new or original theory is to be expected.

The same cannot be said for areas of research in which multiple theoretical perspectives vie for dominance. This is evident in the research on the Fed. Recently, the focus has been less on the specification and elaboration of new theory and more on the testing and evaluation of extant theories. Recent reviews of the monetary policy-making literature tend to focus on issues of measurement and methodology (see Havrilesky 1994; Woolley 1994) and to suggest that the understanding of Fed policy-making should incorporate a wider array of variables and a longer time frame. These are useful suggestions, and they highlight important issues to consider in the development of the understanding of Fed policy-making. They are not, however, the most important issues that currently require resolution. Unfortunately, these issues merely masquerade as those of greatest theoretical importance. In fact, these suggestions implicitly ignore or overlook the fundamental problem inherent in the extant literature: a problem of theory.

I support efforts to conduct empirical tests to evaluate various truth claims. As mentioned previously, my first inclination was to conduct a comprehensive empirical analysis of the various theories of Fed policy-making. Given the diversity of theoretical perspectives, I decided the literature could stand a thorough attempt to evaluate each of the theories and determine which provides the most complete and accurate treatment of Fed policy-making.

Further reading of the literature—and many hours spent thinking about what I was reading—eventually convinced me that my original objective was hopelessly misguided. It became increasingly clear that each of the extant theories provided only a partial explanation of the politics of Fed policy-making. I finally decided that the empirical evaluation of theories would have to wait until a more searching—and thus more revealing—theory could be constructed. In all fairness, I should note that I was not the first to recognize the limitations of the current literature. Munger and Roberts recently concluded that

> the literature . . . suffers from a fundamental lack of integration arising from the lack of an explicit treatment of the overall relation of the Fed to its potential principals. Authors' convictions that they have identified *the* source of political pressure on Fed decision-making all too often lead to ignoring competing hypotheses in the formulation of empirical models. The fact that separate studies have found evidence (however weak) of political influence emanating from disparate sources suggests the strong need for broader, more encompassing studies of the political environment of monetary policy. (1990, 93)

I now turn to this "broader, more encompassing" study of Fed policy-making. Frustration with the eclecticism and varied foci of the extant literature has led me to rethink the theoretical foundations of the study of Fed policy-making, and the results of this rethinking are the substance of this book. However, before moving on to the heart of this work, I must mention two caveats. First, although I develop a new perspective on Fed policy-making, I am admittedly indebted to current theories, both of monetary policy-making and of bureaucratic policy-making more generally. My efforts to move beyond the extant literature assume this literature as a foundation. Second, I do not wish to denigrate empirical study or analysis. This book includes my own efforts to provide empirical support for the theory I espouse, although the book is primarily theoretical. At some point, however, all theories must face the microscope of the real world.

Thus, the desire to develop new theory represented the impetus behind the writing of this book. As I argue in the next chapter and in the remainder of this book, the greatest current obstacle to a more complete understanding of the political dynamics of monetary policy is theoretical. No amount of testing extant theories—regardless of the quality of the data and the sophistication of the methodology—will circumvent or overcome this fundamental shortcoming.

In chapter 2, I review the literature on Fed policy-making. There I discuss the various current perspectives on the political dimensions of monetary policy-making. I also identify the two most important components of any theory of monetary policy-making—explicit treatments of preferences and of institutions—and I evaluate the extent to which each of the current theories incorporates these components. Then, drawing on the bureaucratic policy-making literature, I sketch the outline of a multi-institutional theory that does not suffer from the more significant shortcomings of current perspectives on the politics of monetary policy.

I present the basic multi-institutional theory of Fed policy-making in detail in chapter 3. I describe the assumptions on which the model is based and the characteristics of the model. Chapter 3 also includes a description and explanation of the model's most significant implications. Using the history of monetary policy-making from the end of the Ford administration to the beginning of the Reagan administration, I demonstrate how the multi-institutional model may be used to explain real-world situations. There is also an appendix that contains proofs for the various results presented in the body of the chapter.

In chapter 4, I analyze and discuss the implications of the multi-institutional model when two important assumptions are relaxed: (1) the assumption of constant Fed policy preferences and (2) the assumption of costless congressional action. While the model is somewhat sensitive to relaxation of these assumptions, the basic implications still hold under most circumstances. In general, allowing for shifts in Fed policy preferences or invoking nontrivial (but also nonprohibitive) costs to congressional action does not release the Fed from a need to continue to concern itself with the policy preferences of members of Congress and of the president.

If Fed policy preferences may vary across the range of the policy space and presidents have a significant influence on the character of those preferences through the appointment power, then the basic multi-institutional model might grossly underestimate the president's actual influence on monetary policy-making. Since it is commonly thought that presidents do have the power to manipulate policy via the appointment power, I take up these issues in chapter 5. I consider the appointment process for Fed governors from a multi-institutional perspective, and I evaluate the extent to which the president can utilize appointments to manipulate the Fed's policy preferences. Using a model specifically designed for the appointment process, I attempt to identify those circumstances under which the president's policy preferences are most likely to be reflected in those of an appointee. Using the historical record, I also evaluate the extent to which the number of appointments presidents usually receive—or are sure to receive, from an institutional standpoint—are sufficient to "pack" the Board of Governors or the FOMC.

Chapter 6 provides a more systemic and rigorous empirical analysis of the implications of the multi-institutional model. I discuss some of the difficulties associated with an empirical analysis of multi-institutional models in general and with my model of monetary politics specifically. I demonstrate that the empirical data are consistent with the implications of the multi-institutional model in a way that they are not with regard to other models of monetary policy-making. In short, I find that changes in the policy preferences of the president and Congress have an impact on monetary policy, and these findings are consistent with the multi-institutional model. I also find that several other plausible explanatory schemes, variables, and theories are easily and clearly outperformed by the multi-institutional model.

Chapter 7 brings the multi-institutional model to bear on one of the issues that reaches to the very core of monetary policy-making in a democratic society: the nature of CBI and its impact on policy-making. I will argue that CBI is a multidimensional concept that often complicates rather than clarifies the politics of Fed policy-making. I conclude that the preoccupation with CBI has been misguided or is at least no longer defensible.

In the conclusion, chapter 8, I revisit my findings and briefly discuss their significance for the study of monetary policy-making specifically and bureaucratic policy-making more generally. Ultimately, I discuss the extent to which monetary policy has a democratic character, and I suggest avenues for future research.

CHAPTER 2

The State of the Literature: Looking Back and Looking Ahead

The Fed has fascinated economists and journalists since its creation. Political scientists, latecomers to the study of the Fed, have now demonstrated an interest in the politics of Fed policy-making (see, e.g., Alt 1991; Alt and Woolley 1982; Beck 1982, 1983, 1987, 1990a, 1990b, 1991; Hibbs 1977, 1987; Kettl 1986; Woolley 1984, 1988, 1994). The total body of work on monetary policy is enormous, and research on the political aspects of Fed policy-making is vast in its own right.

Given the size and scope of the literature on the politics of Fed policy-making, its pluralistic character comes as no surprise. Students of monetary policy take a number of different tacks in attempting to describe and explain policy-making at the Fed, quite simply viewing it through a variety of lenses. Unfortunately, at times it appears as if those using one lens are only in the vaguest sense cognizant of the lenses or perspectives of others. The "dialogue" of research on Fed policy-making often involves scholars with radically different perspectives talking past each other.

Though theories of Fed policy-making are quite diverse, each includes—either explicitly or implicitly—the consideration of two fundamental concepts: preferences (of Fed policymakers and other relevant political actors) and constraints on Fed policy choice. These constraints are—either implicitly or explicitly—treated as a function of the policy preferences of other relevant actors in the monetary policy-making arena (usually elected officials) and the institutional structure of the relationship between the Fed and these other actors. To understand why Fed policymakers choose a particular monetary policy—or a particular set of monetary policies over time—one must consider the interrelationships among the policy preferences of Fed policymakers, the policy preferences of other important actors, and the institutional relationship between the Fed and these other actors.[1]

Preferences, Constraints, and Monetary
Policy-Making Institutions

If there is a core theoretical methodology in the literature on the politics of monetary policy-making, it is rational-choice analysis. Of the three major viewpoints on Fed policy-making, two are explicitly within the rational-choice camp (the central bank independence and principal-agent perspectives), and much of the work within the other tradition (the pressure-groups theory) is at least implicitly linked to rational choice methods (see esp. Havrilesky 1995). While theories of monetary policy-making might be constructed on alternative foundations—for example, the psychologically oriented treatments of decision-making dynamics at the Fed (see Havrilesky 1991; Mayer 1990)—the rational-choice perspective is undoubtedly the most prominent theoretical foundation in the current literature.

Rational-choice theory has two fundamental components: preferences and institutions. According to Keech (1995, 17), the "fundamental equation" of public policy-making is the following:

preferences × institutions → outcomes

(See also Plott 1991.) Similarly, Dowding and King note that there are "two important aspects of rational-choice methods in social science: preferences [that] provide the motivation of individual action . . . [and] institutions [that] provide the context allowing causal explanation." And, importantly, these authors go on to argue that rational choice "offers causal explanation of any political outcome *only* where the reasons for individual action are specified, and the structural conditions under which those reasons for action have been modeled are explained" (1995, 1, emphasis added).

Plott's "fundamental equation" implies the following: "If *preferences change,* outcomes can change, even if *institutions remain constant.* If *institutions change,* outcomes can change, even if *preferences remain constant*" (Hinich and Munger 1997, 17). Although the focus of my work deals with the first implication of the fundamental equation—the policy ramifications of changes in preferences in a constant institutional environment—adequate models of Fed policy-making must include a specification of the Fed's policy preferences and a specification of the institutional environment in which the Fed makes its choices. Even if institutions remain unchanged, one must know and understand the specific structure of the institutional environment of monetary policy-making to draw concrete policy implications from the distribution of preferences among the actors involved in the monetary policy arena. The characterization of this environment requires a description of the preferences of the relevant political actors and the character of the institutional relationship between these actors and the Fed. In more straightforward terms, to understand why the Fed does what it does, one must understand what the Fed wants (Fed preferences), what other relevant actors want (their preferences), and what means these other actors have at their disposal for influencing Fed policy activity (the institutional structure of the relationship between the Fed and other actors). The intersection of the policy preferences of actors other than the Fed and the institutional structure of their relationship with the Fed determines the constraints on Fed policy activity. So I will now turn to preferences, constraints, and institutions.

Before going further, however, let me clarify my use of the word *policy*. *Policy* corresponds to *outcomes* in Plott's fundamental equation. For my purposes, it is the Fed's manipulation of a monetary policy instrument—or set of instruments—for a period of time. Thus, policy is assumed to be—as it is in the real world—discretionary. The manifestation of the Fed's policy choice is, however, often an interest rate or other economic variable over which the Fed has no direct control (i.e., the Fed Funds rate). On a conceptual level, the important component of the definition of *policy* is that it excludes policy rules specified by elected officials. A rule-based policy would almost certainly require a significant legislative revision of the amended Federal Reserve Act—a major institutional transformation. While such change is possible, even likely, if the Fed continually ignored the preferences of Congress and the president (see chapter 3), it would also create a very different policy-making environment than the one that currently exists.

Central bankers' preferences are reflected in an ordering of potential policies at a particular point in time. These preferences may depend on a wide variety of factors. Macroeconomic conditions almost certainly play a role in the determination of these policy preferences. For example, an expectation of unusually high future inflation may suggest a very different ordering of potential policies than an expectation of unusually low future inflation. Political factors or circumstances might also play a role in determining the policy preferences of central bankers. In the United States, Democratic presidents tend to appoint more expansionist-minded governors than do Republican presidents (Chappell, Havrilesky, and McGregor 1990, 1993; Woolley 1984). Alt (1991) has suggested that the Fed chairperson's policy preferences vary over the cycle of a four-year chairmanship in such a manner as to maximize the likelihood of reappointment. And several authors have suggested that bureaucratic incentives—such as maximizing agency expenditures—are focal points for explanations of Fed policy preferences (see Toma and Toma 1986 for a survey of this literature).

Central bankers also face a wide variety of constraints when attempting to implement policy choices consistent with their preferences. The nature of the economy may present certain specific constraints. For example, the extent of economic indexation or the presence of a commodity standard such as a gold standard may constrain the extent to which central bankers may implement their optimal policies. Also, the time and resources available for research and policy evaluation are limited, so choices must always be made with the constraint of less-than-perfect information. Even behavioral factors limit the extent to which central banks can achieve policy goals. For example, if individuals accurately anticipate price changes, then the traditional Phillips curve relationship—the trade-off between inflation and unemployment—cannot be exploited in the long run.

Likewise, central bankers may face political constraints in their efforts to achieve their own policy objectives. Specifically, they may face implicit or explicit threats to their autonomy; to avoid these threats, policymakers may be forced to make less-than-optimal policy choices. In the case of the Fed, there are a wide variety of potential policy initiatives that might limit the autonomy or independence of the central bank—annual budgetary appropriations, periodic General Accounting Office audits, investigative hearings, policy targets fixed by Congress, or dissolution of the Fed itself.

It is important to note that these constraints are themselves a function of other factors. The policy preferences of the prominent institutional actors in the monetary policy-making arena, the formal and informal relationship between these actors and the central bank, and the knowledge of the central bank's policy-making activity may each play an important role in the formation of policy constraints.

Monetary policy is, then, at least a function of the preferences of the central bankers and the choice constraints they face. Central bankers' preferences are likely a function of a variety of different factors, including personal and professional background and ideological and partisan disposition. The constraints are a function of the institutional relationship between the central bank and its political environment and the policy preferences of significant actors in it. While a more complete or all-encompassing model of the politics of monetary policy-making might incorporate other factors—for example, informational components—these three factors are the least common denominator of a theory of the politics of monetary policy. An adequate theory of monetary policy-making must include—either explicitly or implicitly—each of these concepts. And, in fact, one can categorize the most prominent theoretical perspectives on the politics of monetary policy by the manner in which each incorporates these concepts.

Woolley (1994) provides a useful description of the three most prominent strands of research in the literature on Fed policy-making. Utilizing his analysis as a starting point, I will now describe and evaluate the embodiment of Fed preferences, institutional structure, and the preferences of other significant actors in each of these theories.

Three Theories of the Politics of Monetary Policy-Making

A.   Central Bank Independence—The Analytical Preeminence of Institutions

Central bank independence and its impact on national economies has become a prominent issue in the macroeconomic literature. According to the literature, significant aspects of CBI include the following: term length of central bankers; appointment and removal procedures for central bankers; extent of budgetary autonomy of the central bank; mechanisms for conflict resolution between central bankers and elected officials; and the existence of formal interest rate, monetary aggregate, or inflation targets (see Cukierman 1992). The results of a number of cross-national studies evaluating the macroeconomic implications of CBI suggest that a direct relationship exists between a central bank's institutional independence and its capacity to maintain price stability (Alesina 1988; Alesina and Summers 1993; Cukierman 1992; Cukierman, Webb, and Neyapti 1991; Grilli, Mascandaro, and Tabellini 1991). Somewhat surprisingly, the relationship between CBI and other macroeconomic variables is unclear (see Alesina and Summers 1993).

While these studies are explicitly comparative, they do have implications for the understanding of Fed policy-making. They consistently rank the Fed as one of the world's most independent central banks. In Cukierman's (1992) 46-country, cross-national ranking of overall CBI, only Denmark and Germany had more independent central banks than did the United States.[2] According to Alesina (1988) and Alesina and Summers (1993), only Switzerland and Germany have more independent central banks. Grilli, Mascandaro, and Tabellini's (1991) ranking system places only Germany's central bank ahead of the Fed in terms of institutional independence. While the methodologies utilized to evaluate levels of independence are quite different, these characterizations of Fed autonomy are consistent with a variety of other writings, ranging from neopopulist polemics (see Greider 1987; Newton 1983) to broad studies of American political institutions (see Knott and Miller 1987; Pious 1979).

The rationale behind the relationship between CBI and stable prices is disarmingly simple. Central bankers, unhesitatingly driven to curtail inflation, naturally prefer monetary policies that maintain, to the extent possible, price stability. Political actors (i.e., the executive and the legislature), conversely, have a variety of incentives to disregard the price-stability objective.[3] Thus, any significant, long-term deviation from price stability is attributed to the capacity of expansionist-minded elected officials to manipulate the policy preferences of the monetary authorities and/or constrain their choice of policies. Long-term price stability implies, therefore, that the central bank is independent of political manipulation and constraint.[4]

How does the CBI theory of monetary policy-making incorporate each of these three explanatory dimensions (Fed preferences, institutional structure, and the preferences of elected officials)? Clearly, the focal point of this literature is institutional. The variables of interest are institutional, and the implicit foundation of this analytical perspective is that variation in the character of monetary policy is a function of variations in the structure of the institutional relationship between central banks and their political environments. Thus, to understand the character of monetary policy, one must understand the institutional environment in which it is made.

Conversely, the policy preferences of central bankers and elected officials are rarely the subject of empirical analysis within this framework. The CBI/institutional literature is founded on two preferential assumptions: (1) elected officials have a consistently strong preference for inflationary policies, and (2) central bankers have consistently strong preferences for price stability. Cukierman (1992) provides the most extensive description of the monetary policy preferences of elected officials. In his view, elected officials have several motivations—increased employment, increased revenue, and a more desirable balance of payments—for their interest and involvement in monetary policy. According to Cukierman, each motive provides an explanation for elected officials' preference for expansionary monetary policy. Elected officials might prefer—at least in the short run—to trade off an increase in inflation for a decrease in unemployment.[5] Likewise, elected officials might attempt to use inflation to boost government revenue through increased seignorage. In essence, Cukierman explains why elected officials prefer inflationary policies. He does not, however, provide any evidence that indicates that elected officials consistently prefer more expansionary policies than do central bankers.

Central bankers are assumed to have an inherent preference for policies that are consistent with price stability. According to proponents of institutional theories of monetary policy-making, when left to their own devices—that is, in a policy-making environment without constraint—

central bankers will always implement policies that are consistent with price stability because they naturally prefer these policies to those that are more expansionary. According to De Carvalho, "The central bank is assumed thus to have an objective function much like consumers and firms, in such a way as to postulate that, left free to act according to its nature, a central bank will fatally and single-mindedly pursue price stability" (1995–96, 164). Banks' inability to maintain price stability is attributed to the imposition of political constraints. Since elected officials consistently prefer expansionary monetary policies, the variance in constraints faced by central banks is a function of the institutional structure of the relationship between the bank and elected officials.

While the CBI theory may provide some theoretical leverage from a cross-national perspective, it has several shortcomings as a theory of the politics of Fed policy-making. First, the assumption that central bankers intrinsically support price stability is problematic. Empirical foundations for this assumption do not exist in the CBI literature, and in the specific case of the Fed, it is clear that the preferences of monetary policymakers vary considerably (see Chappell, Havrilesky, and McGregor 1990, 1993; Havrilesky 1995; Havrilesky and Gildea 1990, 1991, 1992, and 1995; Gildea 1990). It is also clear that differences in preferences are not solely a function of a politicized appointment process. For example, background factors such as educational and professional experience play a role in determining central bankers' policy preferences (Chappell, Havrilesky, and McGregor 1990, 1993; Havrilesky and Gildea 1990, 1991, 1992, and 1995).

The consistency with which elected officials favor expansionary monetary policy is also subject to question in the American case. A significant body of research suggests that Republican presidents tend to favor significantly less expansionary monetary policies than do Democratic presidents (see Havrilesky 1987; Hibbs 1987, 1994; Woolley 1984). Similarly, some literature suggests that presidents' policy preferences change over the course of a term, with a greater preference for expansionary policies near the end of their time in office (Grier 1987, 1989; Haynes and Stone 1989), though the results are less robust than those for the party-differences model (see Alt and Chrystal 1983). The preferences of members of Congress for price stability also tend to differ according to their partisanship and the state of the national economy (see Morris 1995). Thus, at least in the case of the Fed, the assumption that elected officials consistently favor inflationary monetary policies at the expense of price stability is unsubstantiated.

If one is willing to concede that the monetary policy preferences of elected officials and Fed policymakers vary over time, then the role of institutions in the choice of monetary policy becomes more complicated. If both elected officials and Fed policymakers prefer policies consistent with price stability, then it would seem that CBI is no longer a necessary condition for price stability. Likewise, if Fed policymakers favor inflationary policies for reasons unattributable to the pressures or influence of elected officials, then CBI is not sufficient for the maintenance of price stability. Thus, in a world where policy preferences vary, CBI is neither a necessary nor a sufficient condition for the maintenance of price stability. As Woolley argues, "current research shows that no institutional configuration is either necessary or sufficient to guarantee low inflation" (1994, 63). De Carvalho puts it well:

> In sum, both as a theoretical and as an empirical proposition, the connection between independence of the central bank and price stability seems very weak, dependent on very strong and narrow views of how the economy works and what central banks do. (1995–96, 170)

Finally, the theory's preoccupation with formal institutions is particularly problematic in the case of the Fed. The formal (i.e., explicit) institutional structure of the Fed and its relationship with its political environment has been constant since passage of the Federal Reserve Act in 1935. Since that time, the following have remained the same: the size and composition of the Board of Governors and FOMC, the term length of Fed governors, the extent of overlap between the term of the Fed chairperson and the president, the process for nomination of Fed governors, and the process for confirmation of Fed governors. The level of CBI, therefore, provides no analytical leverage for explaining the variance in monetary policies—and in the adherence to the price-stability objective—between 1936 and the present. Therefore, to understand changes in Fed policymaking during this time period it is necessary to look beyond but not ignore the role of formal institutions in the formation of monetary policy.

An understanding of the role of institutional structure on Fed policymaking is undoubtedly an important component to a comprehensive explanation of American monetary policy-making. However, an analytical disregard for the nature of the policy preferences of elected officials and Fed officials limits the explanatory power of the CBI perspective. I do not mean to suggest that formal institutions play no role in the determination of the character of monetary policy. They are, however, only a piece of the puzzle, and one cannot understand or evaluate the effect of formal institutions on the substance of monetary policy without understanding the preferential context in which the central bank exists.

B. Pressure Groups and Fed Policy-Making—
Preferences First

While the CBI perspective focuses explicitly on the impact of institutions on the character of monetary policy, the pressure-group viewpoint centers explicitly on the effect of elected officials' policy preferences on monetary policy-making. In this literature, the institutional environment in which Fed policy-making occurs is treated as relatively unimportant. Kane's (1980, 1982, 1990) "scapegoating" theory, Kettl's (1986) historically oriented treatment of monetary policy-making, and Woolley's work (esp. 1984) fall into this camp, as does more recent work by Havrilesky (1987, 1994, 1995). In fact, Havrilesky's focus is explicitly pressure oriented, as indicated by the title of his last major work, *The Pressures on American Monetary Policy* (1995).[6]

For proponents of the pressure-group theory, the policy preferences of elected officials—most often the president—dominate Fed policy-making. If presidents desire a particular monetary policy, the assumption is that they have the means to obtain Fed compliance, and a substantial literature focuses on the prominence of the president's role in the formation of monetary policy (see Beck 1982; Grier 1987, 1989; Havrilesky 1988, 1995; Hibbs 1977, 1987; Kettl 1986; Williams 1990; Woolley 1984). In support of the significance of the president's policy objectives for Fed policy-making, Hibbs argues that "in practice monetary policy is quite responsive to the political climate, especially as represented by the preferences of the President. This conclusion is supported by virtually every careful analysis of Federal Reserve policy behavior" (1987, 8). Weintraub reaches a similar conclusion, finding that "[w]hat the administration wants or is perceived to want continues to dominate the Federal Reserve's conduct" (1978, 357).

While proponents of the pressure-group perspective may list a number of means by which the president may influence policy—most often signaling (Havrilesky 1988, 1995) and the appointment power (Chappell, Havrilesky, and McGregor 1990, 1993), the path from presidential preferences to policy outcomes is rarely clearly charted. For example, recent research on the appointment power suggests that the ability of presidents to choose governors who share their policy preferences implies that the Board of Governors, as a whole, will share the president's policy preferences (Chappell, Havrilesky, and McGregor 1990, 1993). Nevertheless, other work indicates that a number of factors—term length, potential unreliability, and lack of removal power, among others—prevent presidents from packing the Board of Governors and the FOMC in this manner (Keech and Morris 1997). In sum, Munger and Roberts's (1990) contention that the avenues of influence have not been sufficiently specified is still true, and it is a most apt criticism for the pressure-group perspective.

This is not to say that elected officials eschew efforts to manipulate or influence policy choice. But a theoretical perspective that focuses solely on the preferences of elected officials—and the preferences of other relevant interests—to the exclusion of institutions and Fed preferences is fundamentally incomplete. Consider the following example. At one point, it was suggested to me that Lyndon Johnson, while president, successfully manipulated monetary policy by personally harassing Fed Chairman William McChesney Martin at the president's Texas ranch—another example of the famous Johnson technique.[7] While this story may have some basis in fact, it is difficult, if not impossible, to base a theory of monetary policy-making on the dynamics it describes. Can observers assume that presidents always get their way? A good bit of research suggests that the answer to that question is no (see Beck 1982, 1983, 1987). When do presidents achieve their monetary policy objectives? When they are personally convincing and domineering? Possibly, but how would one go about measuring these qualities? And what if the relationship between the president and Fed chairperson—not to mention the other members of the Board of Governors or the FOMC—depends not only on the personal characteristics of the president but also on the personal characteristics of the chairperson, as Kettl (1986) suggests? The impact of pressure on Fed policy-making then becomes unclear. While these issues could be addressed, proponents of the pressure-group perspective have not done so. Thus, the theoretical foundation of this viewpoint is quite fragile.

C. The Principal-Agent Perspective on Monetary Policy-Making—A First Cut at a Preferential-Institutional Theory

Currently, one of the most prominent theories of Fed policy-making is principal-agent theory (see Alt 1991; Beck 1990b; Caporale and Grier 1993, 1997; Grier 1991; Hetzel 1990; Munger and Roberts 1990; Toma 1991). Principal-agent theory is—first and foremost—an informational theory. A fundamental characteristic of principal-agent theories is the existence of an information asymmetry between principal and agent (see Bendor 1988 and Moe 1984 for an introduction to this vast literature). To the extent that the agents' preferences diverge from those of the principals, agents have incentives to utilize their informational advantages to achieve their goals at the expense of those of the principals. Realizing this potential problem, principals attempt to structure their relationships with agents to minimize (1) the divergence of agent preferences from principal preferences (the problem of adverse selection), and (2) the extent to which agents attempt to achieve their own goals at the expense of the goals of the principal (the problem of moral hazard). First, principals want to avoid choosing agents whose preferences differ significantly from their own. Second, if the preferences of principals and agents do differ, then principals wish to limit the extent to which agents act to achieve goals that are inconsistent with the principals' preferences.

The character of the informational component of the principal-agent relationship is key. If agents have a significant informational advantage, then the problems associated with adverse selection and moral hazard become severe. More generally, as the agent's informational advantage increases, the capacity of the principal to avoid the problems associated with adverse selection and moral hazard decreases.

To limit the extent to which informational asymmetries impose costs on the principal due to agent shirking, principals will choose institutional systems that generate incentive structures that induce agency compliance with principal objectives. Proponents of the principal-agent theory of monetary policy-making make

> a valuable simplifying assumption . . . that the institutional environment in which an agent works has been created deliberately by a principal whose interest the agent is supposed to serve. The incentives in that environment are by definition deliberately created to induce a convergence of the agent's behavior and the interests of the principal. (Woolley 1994, 65)

Given this assumption, changes in agency policy-making should reflect changes in principal preferences, and the institutional structure of the relationship between principal and agent should indicate the means by which the transmission of preferences generates policy change. So, the principal-agent take on monetary policy-making is an attempt to connect institutional structure with the preferences of elected officials and Fed policy-makers.

There are three important strands of thought within the principal-agent perspective toward Fed policy-making: the bureaucratic-independence model, the presidential-control model, and the congressional-dominance model. While each of these principal-agent models shares characteristics with the CBI model of monetary policy-making and the pressure-groups model, the principal-agent models also differ from the other perspectives in theoretically significant ways.

The bureaucratic-independence model of Fed policy-making shares one important component with the CBI perspective on monetary policy-making, namely, the Fed is independent of political manipulation. These two perspectives diverge significantly, however, when it comes to the specification of Fed policy preferences. In the CBI model, the Fed is assumed to desire price stability above all else. In the bureaucratic-independence model, the Fed is assumed to be interested first and foremost in maximizing institutional income—the traditional assumption associated with Niskanen's (1971) bureaucratic budget maximizer. This difference in assumed preferences is extremely important. Even though both the CBI and the bureaucratic-independence models are based on Fed autonomy, the difference in preferences generates different policy outcomes. In the CBI model, the Fed is expected to choose policies that are consistent with price stability. In the bureaucratic-independence model, the Fed is expected to choose policies that maximize Fed revenue. While these policies are not necessarily mutually exclusive, they may often be incompatible.

Some evidence suggests that the Fed attempts to maximize revenue (see Shughart and Tollison 1986; Toma 1982; Toma and Toma 1986). Nevertheless, these results are less than compelling. As Alt notes, none of the evidence indicates that the Fed "generates excessive revenues. In fact, the Fed turns over most of its excess revenue to the Treasury" (1991, 53). If the Fed remits its excess revenue to the Treasury, it is not at all clear why the Fed would have an interest in generating any excess.

Another potential difficulty with the bureaucratic-independence perspective is the manner in which it justifies the "autonomous Fed" assumption. In the CBI literature, a whole host of descriptive institutional analyses support the assumption of Fed independence. In the bureaucratic-independence literature, Fed independence is founded on an assumed informational asymmetry between the Fed and Congress and the president rather than on any explicit institutional analysis. While the Fed may enjoy an informational advantage with regard to its political principals, the extent and significance of this advantage is open to question.

Principal-agent theory's preoccupation with the informational component of the relationship between the Fed and its principal(s) is problematic. The assumption that the Fed has an informational advantage in its "game" with its principal may not be wholly unreasonable. Members of the Board of Governors and the FOMC have long histories of professional experience with matters associated with monetary policy, and the resources and expertise of the Fed's full-time professional staff is often characterized as being second to none in the field of monetary policy. Even so, the informational resources available to the president and members of Congress—particularly in the current "information age"—are substantial. Presidents have a wide range of resources at their disposal—staff with macroeconomic policy-making expertise, the personnel of the Treasury Department, and the Council of Economic Advisors, to name a few—to limit the informational asymmetries that may develop in their relationship with the Fed. There are also important informational resources at the disposal of members of Congress, particularly members of the House and Senate Banking Committees and the Joint Committee on Economic Affairs. GAO audits, more extensive "sunshine" requirements—that is, quicker reporting of the policy outcomes of FOMC meetings—and more significant oversight can also limit whatever informational asymmetries might exist.

Thus, more care must be taken with characterizations of the nature of the informational asymmetries between the Fed and its principal(s). Otherwise, it is possible to confuse "*information-induced* discretion" with "*structure-induced* discretion" (Steunenberg 1996, 311) or preference-induced discretion. Attributing the variance between Fed policy actions and the policy preferences of the president or of members of Congress to the informational dimension of their interrelationships is problematic. While information may play a role in these interactions, it is certainly not necessary to assume an informational advantage on the part of the Fed to explain variance between the Fed's policy actions and the policy preferences of members of Congress and the president. So, even though a number of scholars have identified principal-agent theory as the most likely and most desirable theoretical perspective for the next generation of research—see Alt 1991; Beck 1990a; Hetzel 1990; Toma 1991—its preoccupation with informational asymmetries and the problems associated with the incorporation of multiple principals (not just a president and a unitary-actor Congress, which is difficult, but also a realistic multiactor, bicameral Congress) weigh against its development into a productive theoretical perspective for future analysis of monetary policy-making. The same criticisms can be levied against the use of principal-agent models in the more general analysis of bureaucratic policy-making.

This is not to say that information—and the possibly asymmetric distribution of information—is unimportant. The distribution of information—or, conversely, uncertainty—may well play an important role in the formation of monetary policy-making. Informational asymmetries have played a dominant role in much of the literature on macroeconomic policy-making over the past two decades (see Cukierman and Meltzer 1986; Rogoff 1990; Rogoff and Sibert 1988), and the analysis of the impact of informational asymmetries on monetary policy-making is particularly prominent in the formal literature on the Fed appointment process (see Fratianni, von Hagen, and Waller 1994; Waller 1992; Waller and Walsh 1994).

Nevertheless, preoccupation with the informational component of monetary policy-making prohibits the analysis of the multi-institutional, or intrinsically political, component of monetary policy-making. To the extent that future theoretical endeavors are based on the principal-agent foundation—an informational foundation—they will miss much of the tale that is monetary policy-making. Scholars lack, unfortunately, the methodological or technical apparatus to incorporate an informational component in the most basic of realistic models of policy-making. To do away with the complete and perfect information assumption—that is, to allow some manner of nontrivial uncertainty into the model—would require the simplification of the model through the deletion of various integral components. Discussing the incorporation of an informational component in their own multi-institutional model—one somewhat similar to the model to be presented here—Hammond and Knott note,

> explicit consideration of uncertainty entails mathematical techniques (usefully reviewed in Calvert 1986) which, to make our model tractable, would necessitate simplifications in other aspects of our model, such as a reduction in the number of institutions considered or in the number of individuals in these institutions. . . . this is a tradeoff we are unwilling to make. A multi-institutional model which neglects uncertainty can, we believe, have substantial payoffs, both theoretical and empirical. (1996)

If the bureaucratic-independence model is based on Fed autonomy, the presidential-control and the congressional-dominance versions of the principal-agent treatment of Fed policy-making certainly are not. In fact, both of these models assume preeminence on the part of either the president or Congress and the institutional capacity to assert that preeminence. Both assume that the principal has the capacity to significantly influence policy-making at the Fed.

One example of the presidential-control perspective is Alt's (1991) appointment-based model of Fed-president relations. First, Alt assumes that the president's power of appointment with regard to most of the members of the Board of Governors is relatively unimportant or at least is difficult to use to influence policy. For Alt, the president's ability to appoint the Fed chairperson is of overriding importance. Assuming that the chairperson dominates policy-making at the Fed, and also assuming that chairpersons desire reappointment, Alt concludes that presidents have a means by which they can manipulate Fed policy-making.

This appointment model—even though it includes only two actors, the president and the Fed chairperson—is quite complicated. According to Alt (1991), the presidents' preferences are not always entirely clear, and at certain times the president may not even have preferences about the direction or character of monetary policy. Add to this the fact that presidential terms and the terms of Fed chairpersons are not coterminous, and a situation results in which the chairperson—an individual who is supposedly desperate for reappointment—must decide whether to support the sitting president's policies, the policies of the likely or current challenger, or find some middle ground by "ducking out of the storm." Alt attempts to deal with these complexities, and he presents some evidence that suggests that the empirical record is consistent with the implications of the appointment model.

The congressional-dominance perspective on monetary policy-making is also predicated on the principal's capacity to guide and/or dominate Fed policy-making. The original exposition of the congressional-dominance hypothesis focused on the predominance of subcommittees in the oversight activities of Congress and the relationship between changes in the policy preferences of members of consumer affairs subcommittees in both the House and Senate on changes in Federal Trade Commission policy output (Weingast and Moran 1983). Weingast and Moran argue that the empirical record indicates "that FTC activity is remarkably sensitive to changes in the sub-committee composition" (1983, 793).

Using the framework of the original congressional-dominance model, Grier (1991) evaluates the impact of the ideological composition of the House and Senate Banking Committees on Fed policy-making. His findings and those of Caporale and Grier (1993, 1997) suggest that the changes in the policy preferences of the leadership of the Senate Banking Committee have an impact on policy activity at the Fed; the rate of growth of the monetary base is higher when the Senate Banking Committee is chaired by a liberal than when it is chaired by a conservative.[8]

Both the presidential-influence and congressional-dominance perspectives suffer from important shortcomings. First, although both theories attempt to incorporate institutional structure into the policy-making model, neither provides an adequate depiction of the institutional relationship between the Fed and the president or the Fed and Congress. For example, in the case of Alt's (1991) appointment-oriented model of presidential influence, the Senate's right of confirmation is ignored, and if a president refuses to reappoint the sitting chairperson the new appointee must win confirmation. Just because the president wants to appoint a particular person does not mean that the Senate will confirm that individual, and recent evidence from the Clinton administration suggests that an absence of Senate support for a potential nominee may prevent that individual from being nominated (see Greenwald 1996).

The congressional-dominance theory is equally thin on the institutional particulars of the relationship between the Fed and Congress. Not all theories of congressional oversight imply that committees or subcommittees dominate policy-making, and the original congressional-dominance model was based on a unicameral legislature. While this situation— like the oversimplified characterization of the relationship between the Fed and the president—is not necessarily problematic, it is in this case. Unfortunately, the congressional-dominance results only hold under very specific and exclusive assumptions (see Morris and Munger 1998; Woolley 1993). A more theoretically useful model of the political dimension of Fed policy-making would include a more detailed and complete characterization of the institutional relationship between the Fed and the president and/or the institutional relationship between the Fed and Congress.

This criticism of principal-agent models of Fed policy-making leads to an even more important issue: failure to account for relevant preferences and failure to realize that the Fed has multiple principals. Woolley highlights this problem in his comments on the shortcomings of principal-agent analysis:

> The trap in the principal-agent approach is the possibility that there are multiple principals, each with some power resources, each with different objectives. If there are multiple principles, none of whom is unambiguously dominant, then surely it is a bit of a stretch to begin by *assuming* that the institutional structure they create reflects unambiguously the preferences of any one of them. (1994, 65)

Even when proponents of the various principal-agent models begin to consider the possible existence of multiple principals, they tend to characterize the relationships between the Fed and its principals bilaterally (see Woolley 1994). This suggests that the Fed is either the agent of the president or the agent of Congress. The possibility that the Fed is an agent of both the president and the members of Congress is not considered.

If the Fed is an agent of both the president and Congress, then the straightforward implications of the presidential-control and congressional-dominance theories no longer hold. If the Fed must answer to multiple principals, then it is certainly no longer always independent. Likewise, if the Fed has multiple principals that must coordinate their actions to generate desired outcomes from the Fed, it is clearly not always beholden to either Congress or the president. If the Fed does have multiple principals, then the interrelationships among the members of Congress, the president, and the Fed are more subtle and complex than previously realized.

Moving beyond the Status Quo: A Preface to a
Multi-Institutional Theory of Monetary Politics

According to Dowding and King, "both [preferences] and institutions are important. It would be impossible to explain political behavior and political outcomes without attending to the role that each plays" (1995, 7). This comment highlights the main theoretical shortcoming of the literature on Fed policy-making; not a single extant theory adequately "attends" to the roles of both actors' preferences and institutional structure.

The CBI theory ignores the possibility that preferences may change over time. Elected officials may not uniformly favor monetary expansion, and certain central bankers at certain times may favor monetary policies that are inconsistent with price stability.

The pressure-group's perspective is almost entirely about preferences. Thus, by implication, if one knows the policy objectives of all the relevant players—the members of the FOMC, the president, the members of Congress, professional economists, bankers, members of the Council of Economic Advisors, and so on—it is possible to explain the resulting policy in any specific situation. A single-minded focus on preferences might be reasonable if all actors had equivalent roles and powers, but, at least in the monetary policy-making arena, such is not the case. Likewise, the institutional structure of the relationships among the actors in the monetary policy-making arena gives different actors different rights and responsibilities, and these differences are important.

Finally, the principal-agent perspective deals with both preferences and institutions inadequately. The assumption that the Fed has only a single principal—whether it is the president or Congress—is unnecessarily and erroneously restrictive. Assuming that presidents can mold the institutional structure of their relationship with the Fed without even considering the role of Congress—the institution that must, by law, enact these institutional changes—is also problematic. Likewise, principal-agent models that assume one or a few members of Congress manipulate Fed policy ignore other relevant actors. That the mechanisms through which elected officials influence Fed policy-making have yet to be identified is a testament to the theoretical shortcomings of this perspective.

The past two decades have seen a significant increase in the literature on the politics of monetary policy-making, particularly at the Federal Reserve. Not surprisingly, this body of research has been guided by a variety of different theoretical perspectives. While knowledge of Fed policy-making has advanced, quite possibly due to the diversity of perspectives on monetary policy-making, a snag has been encountered along the way. To advance beyond current understanding, it is necessary to strike out into new theoretical territory. To do so, scholars must be willing to reconsider and reevaluate past assumptions about the preferences of the Fed and other relevant policymakers and about the institutional structure of the relationships between the Fed and these policymakers. What was once taken as given, must now be analyzed. To this end, multi-institutional models of monetary policy-making must be built and used.

In the general policy-making literature, multi-institutional models have become quite popular (see Calvert, McCubbins, and Weingast 1989; Ferejohn and Shipan 1990; Hammond and Knott 1996; Steunenberg 1992, 1996). They provide a theoretical structure within which the preferences of the bureaucracy/regulatory agency, members of Congress, and the president may vary, and they include more realistic characterizations of the structures of the institutional relationships among these actors than earlier models. By providing an analytical tool for dealing with factors that vary—thereby releasing scholars from unrealistically restrictive assumptions—models of this type can provide students of Fed policy-making with the means to a more accurate and more complete understanding of the relevant phenomena than can extant theories. In the next chapter, I lay out the specifics of a multi-institutional model of Fed policy-making.

CHAPTER 3

A Multi-Institutional Theory of Monetary Policy-Making

The controversy over the politics of monetary policy—or the roles that elected officials play in monetary policy-making—is reflected in the more general literature on bureaucratic policy-making. Just as there is no consensus concerning the actual roles of Congress, the president, and the Fed in the arena of monetary politics, there is no consensus concerning the actual roles of Congress, the president, and various bureaucracies in the general arena of bureaucratic politics. Some scholars argue that bureaucracies are independent of manipulation by elected officials. Others see either Congress or the president dominating federal bureaucracies through the lenses of various versions of the principal-agent theory. Still others characterize bureaucracies as pliable institutions that react to changes in the preferences of a host of actors in their political environment.

Proponents of the bureaucratic-independence perspective give a variety of explanations for their contentions concerning the political dimensions of bureaucratic policy-making. Some argue that bureaucracies are independent because elected officials are indifferent toward agency activities and the associated policy outcomes (see Aberbach 1990; Cary 1967; Noll 1971; Ogul 1976; Ogul and Rockman 1990; Rockman 1984; Wilson 1980). As Hammond and Knott note, "[O]ne possible cause of bureaucratic autonomy is simply the indifference of those who have the authority to do something about it" (1996). Likewise, students of the Fed have long argued that members of Congress are not active and effective players in the monetary policy-making arena because of their lack of interest (see Weintraub 1978; Beck 1990a).

Another reason for bureaucratic independence is the informational advantages that accrue to bureaucracies. If members of Congress and the president have an inaccurate or incomplete understanding of the policy-making activities of federal agencies, they will find it difficult to manipulate or influence agency activities. Particularly when agencies work in policy areas that are especially complex—or when agency outputs are difficult to measure or identify—the capacity of the agency to avoid effective oversight is considerable. A number of scholars have investigated the impact of these informational asymmetries on the relative independence of federal agencies (Banks 1989; Banks and Weingast 1992; Bendor, Taylor, and Van Gaalen 1987; Miller and Moe 1983; Niskanen 1971). According to proponents of principal-agent theory, the complexity of monetary policy might also foster the development of informational asymmetries between the Fed and its principals (see Beck 1990a).

Finally, some scholars argue that the nature of the institutional relationship between federal bureaucracies, Congress, and the president makes it difficult for either Congress or the president to unilaterally manipulate policy. Career bureaucrats—like Fed governors—are difficult if not impossible to remove from office. Both the Senate and the president must agree on the acceptance of new bureaucratic leaders. Furthermore, federal agencies can issue regulations and rules that have the force of law without the direct and explicit prior approval of either house of Congress or the president, thereby limiting the extent to which elected officials can influence bureaucrats' policy-making activity, particularly when members of Congress and the president do not agree on a particular issue of policy. The institutional structure of the relationships among Congress, the president, and agencies makes manipulation difficult.

As there are proponents of the principal-agent perspective toward Fed policy-making, there are champions of the principal-agent perspective for analyzing the relationship between Congress and various bureaucratic agencies and the president and various bureaucratic agencies. The congressional-dominance hypothesis implies that a principal—usually a congressional committee—is able to control the policy output of the federal agency in the committee's area of purview. The theory also suggests that this control will be implicit (that is, agencies will react to changes in congressional policy preferences without the overt use of congressional force). So even if Congress does not appear to be conducting oversight or manipulating an agency, the threat of sanction alone is sufficient to generate agency compliance. This theory has been used to analyze the Federal Trade Commission (Calvert, Moran, and Weingast 1987; Weingast and Moran 1982, 1983), the Securities and Exchange Commission (Weingast 1984), and the Federal Reserve (Grier 1991). More general treatments of the congressional-dominance perspective include Bendor, Taylor, and Van Gaalen (1987), Lupia and McCubbins (1994), McCubbins and Schwartz (1984), McCubbins (1985), and Weingast (1981).

Other treatments of bureaucratic policy-making contend that the president plays the role of principal to the bureaucracy's agent. Several studies explicitly describe the relationship between president and bureaucracy in principal-agent terms (Cook and Wood 1989; Ringquist 1995;

Waterman 1989; Wood 1988; Wood and Waterman 1991). There are also those who view the president as the preeminent player in the arena of bureaucratic policy-making who do not make explicit use of the principal-agent perspective (Eisner and Meier 1990; Moe 1982, 1985; Nathan 1983; Scholz and Wei 1986; Wood and Anderson 1993). Though this work does not include the usual principal-agent jargon, it still falls within the broad outlines of principal-agent theory.

In much of the literature that focuses on the relationships between the president and various federal bureaucracies, the president's power of appointment is identified as the tool that is most useful in helping the executive achieve policy goals (Moe 1985; Nathan 1983; Waterman 1989; Wood and Anderson 1993; Wood and Waterman 1991, 1993). This contention certainly makes sense in a principal-agent framework. If a principal can choose an agent with similar policy preferences, informational asymmetries become relatively unproblematic. At the least, shirking is minimized. Shirking or moral hazard problems only make sense in a context in which there is a significant difference between the preferences of the agent and those of the principal. This preoccupation with the appointment power is also reflected in the literature on Fed policy-making. Several scholars have identified the appointment power as the central mechanism through which presidential preferences influence the Fed (Chappell, Havrilesky, and McGregor 1990, 1993; Havrilesky and Gildea 1990, 1991, 1992, 1995).

Several studies of bureaucratic policy-making suggest that a whole host of actors influence agencies' policy activity and their policy outputs. Wilson's (1989) work on bureaucratic policy-making includes treatments of the relationships among Congress, the president, the courts, interest groups, and federal agencies. He suggests that the political context within which bureaucracies mold policy is complex and that bureaucracies react to a variety of significant stimuli. Moe's (1987) critique of the congressional-dominance hypothesis indicates that a complete description of bureaucracies' political environments would include a multitude of political actors. Likewise, other work by Moe (1985) also indicates that bureaucracies pay attention to a variety of political actors (Congress, the president, and the courts).

This line of research resembles the pressure-group's perspective taken by some students of Fed policy-making (see, e.g., Havrilesky 1995). Bureaucracies are assumed to have complex political environments, and sophisticated quantitative analyses are often utilized to demonstrate that bureaucratic outputs are correlated with a variety of political stimuli. However, as in the case of the pressure-group theorists, little effort is made to describe the interactive nature of the agency's relationship with its political environment, and clear specification of the variety of mechanisms through which the actors exercise their influence is nonexistent.

Finally, a relatively recent strain of research on bureaucratic policy-making uses the conceptual structure of principal-agent theory to explain the relationship between bureaucracies and their political environments—environments that are assumed to include multiple principals: the president, various congressional committees, the courts, the news media, and interest groups (see Wood and Waterman 1993, 1994). Characteristically, these studies include an overview of principal-agent theory. These summaries focus on the advantages that accrue to agencies due to informational asymmetries and the capacity of the various principals to mold the agency's political environment to diminish the problems associated with informational asymmetries. Research in this vein often includes a feedback loop through which the agency can actually influence the policy preferences and activities of the principals.

While the quantitative analyses incorporated in these studies is sophisticated, the theoretical foundations of the research are fragile. Principal-agent theory is designed to explain the strategic dimension of the interrelationship between a single principal and a single agent. It is not at all clear—and these studies make no attempt to demonstrate—that the implications of principal-agent theory hold when the policy-making environment includes multiple principals. A recent review of Wood and Waterman's *Bureaucratic Dynamics: The Role of Bureaucracy in a Democracy,* an exemplar of this strain of scholarship, puts it succinctly:

> The notion of competing, *multiple principals,* endorsed by Moe [1984] . . . and the present authors (pp. 147–149), seems nonsensical from the point of view of the original [principal-agent] model. Thus, it is reasonable to conclude that the existence of competing principals invalidates a chief assumption of the principal-agent model and makes it inappropriate for application to the problem of political control of bureaucracy at the macro level. Using principal-agent jargon when the theoretical underpinnings for its use are absent does not contribute to political analysis. (Hill 1995, 771)

One cannot merely assume that the dynamics of the principal-agent model will hold when multiple principals are incorporated. That the empirical analysis indicates that bureaucracies react to a variety of political stimuli does not mean that the dynamic is the one identified by the original principal-agent model.

As in the case of the Fed, some scholars argue that federal bureaucracies are independent, some argue that bureaucracies are in a principal-agent relationship with either Congress or the president, and some contend that a multitude of important actors influence bureaucratic policy-making. In an effort to provide a theoretical resolution to this controversy in the literature, several scholars have constructed multi-institutional models of bureaucratic policy-making (see Calvert, McCubbins, and Weingast 1989; Eskridge and Ferejohn 1992; Ferejohn and Shipan 1990; Hammond and Knott 1996; Huxtable 1994; Spitzer 1990). Proponents of this type of analysis attribute its usefulness to the inclusion of a comprehensive set of institutional actors; they presume the implications of their multi-institutional models have a certain face validity that more limited models do not (see Hammond and Knott 1996).

If multi-institutional models provide insight into the general nature of bureaucratic policy-making, they can also provide insight into the nature of monetary policy-making. In this chapter, I develop a model of monetary policy-making that fills a significant gap in the current literature on the relationship between the Fed and its political environment, and I work through several of the more important implications of the model. The model, one which is strongly influenced by the most recent multi-institutional literature on regulatory/bureaucratic policy, provides a theoretical framework for understanding the interrelationship among the policy preferences of elected officials, the policy preferences of the Fed, and the institutional relationship between the Fed and its political environment. This model provides a theoretical rationale for understanding the relationship between the policy preferences of elected officials and the Fed's policy activity, and it will aid in the understanding of the mechanisms through which elected officials influence Fed policy activity. The model also provides a useful guide to the empirical analysis of political pressures on monetary policy.

While I use multi-institutional theory to understand the politics of monetary policy, this focused use of the theory in a specific context also contributes to the more general literature on bureaucratic policy-making. Although multi-institutional models of policy-making are becoming increasingly popular, rigorous empirical tests of the implications of specific models are quite rare. As previously noted, proponents of these models justify their relative validity—as compared to simpler principal-agent models—by highlighting the greater verisimilitude of their assumptions (see, for example, Hammond and Knott 1996). One should, however, be wary of evaluating a theory on the basis of assumptions alone (Friedman 1953).

Policy-making at the Fed is a very special case of bureaucratic policy-making. Admittedly, it is an unusual regulatory agency. Nevertheless, the case of the Fed can be very useful for the testing of a multi-institutional theory of bureaucratic politics. Since the Fed is so unusual—and because multi-institutional theories were designed to address the political character of more conventional bureaucracies—the Fed is a particularly difficult case for the validation of multi-institutional theory. In essence, the case of the Fed is a least-likely case for the testing of a multi-institutional theory of bureaucratic politics (see Eckstein 1975).[1] From a theoretical standpoint, the failure of multi-institutional theory to provide an adequate explanation of the political character of Fed policy-making would not be particularly damning. How could one denigrate a theory for failing to explain an admittedly abnormal or unusual case? However, if multi-institutional theory does provide important insight into the politics of Fed policy-making—an application for which this theory was not specifically designed—it should instill confidence that the theory will provide even greater insight into the nature of bureaucratic politics in agencies that have more conventional characteristics. Again, while my specific focus is monetary policy, this analysis also has implications for the study of bureaucratic policy-making in general.

Preliminaries to a Multi-Institutional Model of Monetary Policy-Making

Although I introduce only one model of monetary policy-making in this chapter, I present that model in two stages of institutional verisimilitude. I begin with a multi-institutional model that includes members of Congress, the president, and the Fed. In this model I treat Congress as a unicameral body. A subsequent version of the model will deal with the complexities introduced with the inclusion of a second house of Congress.

I construct this model of monetary policy-making in unidimensional space. Although there are extant models of bureaucratic policy-making that are both multi-institutional in scope and multidimensional in nature (see Kiewiet and McCubbins 1991; Hammond and Knott 1996), monetary policy-making appears to be particularly well suited for unidimensional analysis. While monetary politics is certainly complex, it is not clear that the payoff associated with modeling in a multidimensional space would be worth the cost in added complexity. It is a convention for those studying monetary policy to write of monetary "ease" and monetary "tightness," of more expansionary monetary policy and more restrictive monetary policy. Ease and tightness are clearly captured in a single dimension, and it is not obvious what other aspects of monetary policy-making would be captured with additional dimensions.

In this model, the Fed alone determines monetary policy. I do, however, assume that the Fed is sensitive to the potential costs associated with the implementation of any particular monetary policy and that the Fed will not choose a particular policy if this choice will initiate congressional reprisal. Thus, the influence of Congress is exercised through its ability to punish the Fed for undesirable policy actions. Conversely, the president's influence on monetary policy is exercised through the ability to prevent congressional sanction.

Initially, the Fed's ideal policy position is set to correspond to the price stability goal or objective. This is consistent with the contention in the central bank independence (CBI) literature that central bankers have an intrinsic disposition toward monetary conservatism (Cukierman 1992). I relax this assumption in the next chapter.

Two Versions of a Multi-Institutional Model of Monetary Policy-Making

Assume that the Fed, the president, and Congress (unicameral, at this point) have ideal policy positions in a unidimensional policy space. Let the policy space be characterized by a line segment, with the left end of the line segment corresponding to extreme monetary ease and the right end of the line segment corresponding to extreme monetary tightness or perfect price stability. Let F stand for the ideal policy position of the Fed, which will rest at the right extreme of the line segment or the right frontier of the policy space. Let P represent the ideal policy position of the president. Let C represent the ideal policy position of the Congress, which would—in this unidimensional environment—correspond to the ideal policy position of the median member of Congress in this policy space.[2] Finally, let O represent the boundary points for an effective presidential veto.

This game is sequential in nature. Initially, the Fed chooses a policy position. Then Congress decides whether to sanction the Fed. If Congress enacts a sanction, the president either vetoes or does not veto the bill. Finally, if the president vetoes the sanction, Congress either does or does not override the presidential veto. Assuming that the Fed wishes to avoid punishment and that all actors have complete and perfect knowledge of the policy preferences of all other actors, the Fed will choose that position in the policy space that is closest to F and still avoids congressional sanctions. The Fed can avoid punishment in two ways:

1. Choose the ideal policy position of Congress as the actual policy position.
2. Choose a policy position that is not the ideal policy position of Congress but is both
   a. closer to the president's ideal policy position than to the ideal policy position of Congress, and
   b. on or within the override boundaries.

Thus, Congress will always punish the Fed for choosing a policy position outside the override boundaries.

Exactly why Congress will punish the Fed for implementing a policy outside the override boundaries is not immediately obvious; however, there is an intuition behind this result. Suppose the Fed chooses a policy position beyond the override boundaries that will not elicit congressional reprisal. In this case, there exists, by definition, a policy position preferred by at least two-thirds of Congress to the position chosen by the Fed. When such is the case, it is reasonable to expect the sponsorship of a proposal in Congress to sanction the Fed through congressional policy-setting. To presume that the Fed could avoid sanction after choosing a policy so clearly inconsistent with the preferences of so many members of Congress certainly implies that the bulk of its membership would, on a regular basis, behave in an irrational manner.

Assuming none of the actors wish to have their actions negated (i.e., Congress wants to avoid a successful veto and the president wants to avert an override), the solution concept for this game is a subgame perfect equilibrium (see Ferejohn and Shipan 1990; Spitzer 1990; Steunenberg 1992 for uses of this solution concept in similar settings). Thus, none of the actors will, in equilibrium, take actions off the equilibrium path (i.e., the president will never issue a veto that Congress can override). Thus, in equilibrium, we would never expect Congress to sanction the Fed. As in the congressional-dominance literature, the inactivity of Congress does not indicate its irrelevance to or impotence in the policy-making process (see Weingast 1984; Weingast and Marshall 1988; Weingast and Moran 1983). The same is true for the president. Ferejohn and Shipan describe this important aspect of multi-institutional models:

> [I]n settings with complete information, in equilibrium the initial agency policy is never overturned. Thus, actual legislation never occurs. The agency takes an action and Congress simply accepts it. Second, the equilibrium agency proposal depends on congressional and [presidential preferences.] In this sense, Congress is influential in agency policy without taking action, [as is the president]. (1990, 7)

Clearly, the multi-institutional model is a game among Congress, the Fed, and the president, and the game occurs in stages.

Consider this scenario:

———O1———C———O2—F,P   Fig. 3.1

In figure 3.1, the Fed and the president have the same ideal point: both the Fed and the president want complete price stability. According to the party-differences model of macroeconomic politics, this position is not particularly unusual for a Republican president (see Hibbs 1987; Alesina and Rosenthal 1989).

In figure 3.1, the equilibrium actual policy position will correspond to override position O2. The Fed cannot designate as an actual policy position any point in the policy space that is to the right of O2 without incurring legislative punishment. O2 is the point in the policy space nearest to the Fed's ideal policy position that the Fed can choose as an actual policy position and still avoid congressional punishment. The intuition behind this result is as follows. Suppose that the Fed chooses a policy position beyond O2. In that case, if some congressional agenda setter proposes a policy closer to his or her own ideal policy—for example, just to the right of O2—then that proposal will defeat the status quo of the Fed's choice, F, and any presidential veto will be defeated. The only way that the Fed can avoid being rolled in this manner is to choose a policy no farther to the right than O2. If the policy choice is to the right of O2, then a congressional agenda setter can always propose O2 and carry the day. If the policy choice is O2, no veto-proof alternative defeats the Fed's policy position. So, to expect the Fed to successfully implement a policy more conservative than O2 is tantamount to assuming—in the context of the current game—that the members of Congress are behaving irrationally.

Now consider the scenario presented in figure 3.2.

P———O1———C———O2—F   Fig. 3.2

The sole distinction between the scenarios in figures 3.1 and 3.2 is the change in the ideal policy position of the president. In figure 3.1, the president and the Fed had exactly the same ideal policy position. In figure 3.2, the ideal policy positions of the president and the Fed are at opposite ends of the policy space. From the perspective of the party-differences theory of macroeconomic politics, this is not a particularly unusual positioning of the actors' preferences if the president is a Democrat. One would expect a Democratic president to focus on growth stimulation at the expense of price stability, and one would expect a Congress composed of both Republicans and Democrats to have an ideal policy position somewhere between the extreme emphasis on price stability of the Fed and the extreme emphasis on growth stimulation of the president (see Alesina, Londregan, and Rosenthal 1993; Alesina and Rosenthal 1989).

The equilibrium outcome in figure 3.2 is clearly different from the equilibrium outcome in figure 3.1. In figure 3.2, the Fed will choose as the actual policy position point C, the ideal policy position of Congress. The Fed has no incentive to choose a policy position to the left of C, and any actual policy position to the right of C will be met with legislative sanction.

In this case, the president has no incentive to threaten a veto so that the Fed might designate O2 as the actual policy position.

Now consider figure 3.3.

——O1*—O1————C*—C————O2*—O2—F,P   Fig. 3.3

Figure 3.3 is an exact copy of figure 3.1, except for the addition of the O1*, C*, and O2* notation. Remembering that O2 is the equilibrium policy position in figure 3.1, what is the equilibrium policy position if the congressional ideal point and the two override points move to positions O1*, C*, and O2*? If these movements are made, it is easy to see that the new equilibrium policy position will be O2*. Suppose the same movements of C, O1, and O2 occur in the scenario presented in figure 3.2. In this case, the equilibrium position still moves, but instead of moving from O2 to O2* it moves from C to C*.

Although this is an admittedly simple model, it provides some important insight into the political dynamics of the formation of monetary policy. First, this model implies that the extent of Fed independence depends—in an important way—not only on the institutional structure of the monetary policy arena but also on the policy preferences of elected officials. As shown previously, the proximity of the equilibrium policy position to the Fed's ideal policy position—and thus the extent of Fed independence—depends on the policy preferences of both the president and Congress. In addition, the model provides an institutionally sensitive explanation for why the policy preferences of both Congress and the president might have an impact on monetary policy. Alesina and Rosenthal (1989) and Alesina, Londregan, and Rosenthal (1993) argue that macroeconomic policy outcomes depend on the partisanship of the president and the balance of partisan power in Congress. If the party-differences theory provides an explanation for presidential and congressional policy preferences, then this model provides an explanation for why both the partisanship of the president and the partisan balance in Congress have an impact on monetary policy-making.

This model also provides an interesting explanation for the empirical relationship between presidential policy preferences and the substance of monetary policy. Suppose Congress's ideal policy position is very close to that of the Fed. How much would one expect presidential policy preferences to affect Fed policy-making? Figures 3.4 and 3.4A illustrate that situation.

————————————O1—C—O2-F,P   Fig. 3.4

P————————————O1—C—O2—F   Fig. 3.4A

In figure 3.4, the equilibrium policy position is at point O2. In the scenario in figure 3.4A, the equilibrium policy position is at point C. Even though the president's ideal policy position moved from one extreme point to the other in the policy space, the equilibrium policy position only moved the short distance from point O2 to point C. In this model, the closer Congress's policy preferences are to those of the Fed, the less the impact of changes in presidential policy preferences. Historically speaking, at least over the past 40 years, it is quite likely that Congress's policy preferences have not been particularly close to those of the Fed (given the Democratic control of Congress for much of the time period), and, thus, the movement in presidential policy preferences has had a greater impact on Fed policy-making than it would have if congressional policy preferences and Fed policy preferences had been in concert.

A more institutionally accurate model of monetary policy-making would include policy preferences for both houses of a bicameral Congress (figure 3.5). In this version of the basic model, the ideal policy position of Congress (C) will be replaced by the ideal policy positions of the House (H) and Senate (S). The original veto override points (O1 and O2) will be replaced by veto override points for both the House (HO1 and HO2) and Senate (SO1 and SO2). The ideal policy positions for the Fed and the president will be characterized in exactly the same manner as before.

—SO1————HO1—S—H—SO2————HO2————F,P   Fig. 3.5

Realizing that a successful veto override requires the support of both houses of Congress, the equilibrium policy position in this scenario is at the point HO2. The Fed has no incentive to choose any point to the left of point HO2 as the actual policy position, and if the Fed chooses any point to the right of the policy point HO2, it will incur a legislative sanction.

If the president's ideal policy position moves to the left extreme of the policy space, the policy point H becomes the equilibrium policy position (see figure 3.6).

P—SO1————HO1—S—H—SO2————HO2-———F   Fig. 3.6

The Fed cannot choose an actual policy position to the right of H without incurring legislative punishment, and—given the fact that the Fed can choose H as the actual policy position and avoid punishment—it has no incentive to choose any policy position to the left of H.

TABLE 3.1. Monetary Policy and the Effect of Shifts in Presidential and Congressional Preferences

	Fed Response To:		
Scenario	Shift in Presidential Preferences	Shift in Senate Preferences[a]	Shift in House Preferences
P < S < H < F	Corresponding shift in policy	No policy change	Corresponding shift in policy
P < H < S < F	Corresponding shift in policy	Corresponding shift in policy	No policy change
S < H < P,F	Corresponding shift in policy	No policy change	Corresponding shift in policy
H < S < P,F	Corresponding shift in policy	Corresponding shift in policy	No policy change

[a]I assume that the shift in chamber preferences is not large enough to change the ordering of congressional preferences (i.e., the more conservative house prior to a shift is also the more conservative house after the shift).

The implications of the multi-institutional model indicating the relationship between shifts in preferences and shifts in policy are summarized in table 3.1. Assuming a distribution of preferences—that is, the preferences of the president, members of Congress, and the Fed are specified and depicted in the policy space—the multi-institutional model provides, at least theoretically, the means to predict how changes in the preferences of members of Congress and/or the president will impact policy formation at the Fed.

Table 3.1 provides a summary of the predicted relationship between changes in policy preferences and changes in policy. For example, suppose the distribution of preferences is characterized by P < S < H < F. In this scenario, a change in the Senate's policy preferences—that is, the policy preferences of the median voter in the Senate shift but do not become more liberal than those of the president or more conservative than those of the median voter in the House—will not have any impact on policy. If the preferences of the median voter in the Senate change to the point that they are actually more conservative than those of the median voter in the House, the implications of figure 3.1 are correct up to the point that S moves to the other side of H. At this point, the implications associated with the P < H < S < F scenario are relevant, and a corresponding tightening of monetary policy would be expected.

So, in general, the Fed responds to shifts in the policy preferences of (1) the president and (2) the more conservative chamber of Congress. The multi-institutional model implies that the Fed will pay no attention to the changes in the policy preferences of the more liberal—or more expansionist-minded—chamber of Congress.[3]

In addition to relating changes in the preferences of elected officials to policy changes, the multi-institutional model highlights a more general phenomenon: the relationship between the variance of the preferences among members of Congress and congressional influence over policy. Imagine a situation in which there is no preferential variance among members of Congress: all override positions and both median voter positions would occupy exactly the same point in the policy space. Under these circumstances, the multi-institutional model indicates that the relationship between congressional preferences and policy is perfect—what Congress wants, Congress gets. This situation exemplifies the congressional-dominance hypothesis, and the multi-institutional model implicitly suggests that the extent to which Congress influences or controls monetary policy-making is a function of the variance in congressional policy preferences.

Now, of course, all members of Congress having the same policy preferences would be very unusual. The size of the House and the size of the Senate practically prohibit the perfect correspondence of all legislators' policy preferences. Nevertheless, this dynamic is an important one to understand. As congressional preferences become more cohesive, the institution's capacity to achieve its own policy objectives—as manifested by the policy preferences of the median voters—becomes greater. Simply put, agreement fosters power.

Also, by *agreement* I do not simply mean the relationship between the median voters' ideal points; I am also referring to the correspondence between the opposing override voters in each chamber. The preoccupation with the dynamics of divided government has obscured the relative importance of within-chamber variance in bureaucratic policy-making environments. Even if both chambers have identical medians, large variance in a single house can provide the Fed—and other bureaucratic agencies—with the opportunity to achieve its own policy objectives. (For a more detailed treatment of this dynamic, which is not unique to the arena of monetary policy, see Morris and Munger 1998.)

A Case Study: The Political Dynamics of Monetary Policy-Making, 1974–1981

Models are, by their very nature, simplifications of reality; they tell only a portion of the empirical story. But if a model has explanatory power, then it may teach something important. Not surprisingly, I argue that the multi-institutional model—even in its most basic form—provides a useful perspective on the nature of monetary policy-making and bureaucratic policy-making more generally.

The following chapters extend the model to more general circumstances or situations (chapter 4), evaluate an important alternative perspective toward monetary policy-making (chapter 5), present an extensive multivariate empirical analysis of the implications of the model (chapter 6), and identify the new insights that the multi-institutional model provides into one of the most interesting issues in the study of monetary policy-making—the relationship between CBI and price stability (chapter 7). The remainder of this chapter is a relatively simple case study, a brief analysis of the political dynamics of Fed policy-making from the Ford administration to the beginning of the Reagan years. My objective is to demonstrate how the multi-institutional model can be used to understand specific instances of real-world policy-making, particularly in those instances in which competing models fall short.

The first portion of the time period (late 1974 to late 1976) is the years of the Ford administration. This era provides an example of a situation in which the conservative, tight-money preferences of the president provided protection for the Fed's resistance to the expansionary pressure exerted by Congress. Facing a potential presidential veto, Congress found it difficult to successfully sanction the Fed for the restrictive monetary policy it implemented during the Ford administration.

The second portion of the time period covers the Carter administration. The experience of the Carter administration highlights the limitations on Fed independence when both Congress and the president favor an expansionary monetary policy. But this period also demonstrates that even when presidential policy preferences remain constant, the Fed will still react to shifts in congressional policy preferences. The first two years of the Carter presidency offer an excellent example of a situation in which both Congress and the president favored more inflationary policies than did the Fed. The last two years of the Carter administration, conversely, witnessed increasing conservatism in monetary policy, a direct, if subtle, reaction to a shift in the policy preferences in Congress and specifically in the Senate.

Finally, I examine the beginning of the Reagan administration, a period in which the tight-money conservatism of the president and the first Republican-controlled Senate in nearly 30 years produced the most restrictive monetary policy in recent memory. As the multi-institutional model suggests, with a president and a significant portion of at least one chamber of Congress on its side, the Fed can go a long way toward achieving its own policy goals.

The President as Protector: Ford and the Fed

According to Havrilesky, "On five occasions in this century Congress has effectively asserted its authority over the management of monetary policy" (1995, 113).[4] One of these instances occurred during the Ford administration, at the time of the passage of House Concurrent Resolution 133 (113). HR 133 was considered by many to be one of the most important legislative reactions to what many members of Congress considered an unnecessarily restrictive monetary policy. As a major policy initiative, it was widely expected to have an immediate impact on the character of monetary policy. As Kettl argues, HR 133 "was a watershed in Fed-congressional relations" (1986, 146). Although it is possible that over the long term, the role of Congress in the formation of monetary policy changed after 1975, the immediate impact of HR 133 was quite limited. Simply put, the congressional interest in monetary policy that eventually led to the passage of HR 133 was a direct result of the Fed's relatively restrictive monetary policy—a policy supported by President Gerald Ford. And Ford's support, along with that of a significant number of conservative-minded legislators, restricted HR 133's immediate impact on policy.

Few, if any, American presidents in the postwar era were more supportive of Fed independence than was Ford.[5] According to Kettl, Ford "respected the Fed's independence from the White House" (1986, 132). Kettl cites then-chairman Arthur Burns in support of this observation, "Every President I have known has made remarks about the independence of the Federal Reserve. Gerry Ford believed it. [It was] part of his 'political religion'" (132). Ford's support for the Fed's independence coexisted happily with his penchant for fighting inflation. In fact, the foundation for Ford's support of Fed independence was the congruence between Fed policy objectives (price stability) and his own policy preferences.

Ford's desire to fight inflation is legendary. Havrilesky indicates that the "Ford Administration's anti-inflationary militance was well known" shortly after the president took office (1995, 62). Ford initiated the WIN (Whip Inflation Now) campaign, with its promotional red buttons, and according to Hibbs, this campaign—and Ford's general anti-inflationary leanings—led to "the most severe contraction since the Great Depression of the 1930s" (1987, 74). Kettl contends that "Burns' unflinching tight money policy won quiet applause" from the Ford administration (1986, 134). It is possible to argue that Ford's WIN campaign was never a serious political program, but even so, its symbolic relevance is undeniable, and it surely reflects Ford's own macroeconomic predilections.

Given Ford's interest in fighting inflation, the relationship between the Fed and the president during his administration was unusually close; at least one student of monetary policy-making argues that Ford and Burns had "the closest relationship between a president and a Fed chairman in history" (Kettl 1986, 132). According to Kettl, the Fed and the Ford administration "developed an extraordinarily close relationship and worked together to try to break the inflation strangling the American economy. The Fed and the administration had rarely spoken so much with one voice or worked with such subtle cooperation" (1986, 136). There is little evidence suggesting that any significant conflict between the Fed and the administration existed during the Ford years, a remarkable circumstance in and of itself (Woolley 1984, 124).

While the president and the Fed saw eye to eye between late 1974 and late 1976, Congress and the Fed were often at loggerheads. Chairman Burns had a historically poor relationship with the Congress. According to Kettl, Burns's "confrontations with members of Congress were legendary [and his] conflicts with Congress became the sharpest in Fed history" (1986, 140–41). As Havrilesky notes, "Never before had the Fed come under such congressional attack" (1995, 111). While one might attribute some of the tension between the Fed and Congress to Burns's contentious personality, the core of the conflict among Congress, the Fed chairperson, and the Fed itself had its foundation in the poor state of the national economy. The uncommonly high interest rates were particularly problematic (see Kettl 1986; Woolley 1984). Members of Congress apparently reacted to these excessively high interest rates and pressured the Fed to ease monetary policy and lower interest rates (Alt 1991; Kettl 1986; Woolley 1984).

In this situation, the president was protecting the Fed from the loose-money pressures of Congress. Consider the configuration of preferences in figure 3.7:

——O1——C——O2——P,F   Fig. 3.7

Because of the threat of a presidential veto, Congress will not sanction the Fed as long as it chooses a monetary policy that corresponds to the ideal policy position of Congress, the O2 override position, or any policy position between these two points. Given the Fed's desire to minimize the distance between the actual policy position and its ideal policy position, subject to the constraint of legislative sanction, the Fed is predicted to choose the position that corresponds to O2. Without the protection of the president—in this case, Ford—the Fed would be forced to give in to congressional pressure for significant monetary expansion.

During the Ford administration, the shared policy objective of fighting inflation provided the foundation for a relationship between the president and the Fed that allowed it to choose a monetary policy that was significantly more restrictive than Congress wanted. Here the ability of the president to protect the Fed through the threat or use of the veto provided cover and protection for the Fed to resist congressional pressure to ease monetary policy.

Ganging up on the Fed: The Early Carter Years

With Carter's election, the Fed lost the presidential protection it enjoyed during the Ford administration. Carter's monetary policy preferences were considerably more expansionary than those of the inflation-averse Ford. As the policy preferences of Congress were still leaning toward monetary expansion, the Fed had no choice but to institute a significantly more expansionary monetary policy in 1977.

The first year of Carter's presidency is widely characterized as a time during which the president desired very expansive monetary policies and heavily pressured the Fed to enact those policies.[6] Ford clearly considered a low level of inflation preferable to a low level of unemployment if forced to choose between the two, but, as Hibbs argues, Ford's "priorities were reversed during the first years of the Carter administration, which emphasized the traditional Democratic party goal of moving the economy toward full employment" (1987, 74). An essential component of Carter's macroeconomic program was an "easier monetary policy to keep interest rates down" (Kettl 1986, 167). Clearly, "The Carter Administration adhered faithfully to . . . inflationary low interest rates" (Havrilesky 1995, 63). During the first two years of the Carter presidency, the administration's preferences were so adamantly tied to an expansionary monetary policy that all 29 administration signals to the Fed during that time period were for ease (see Havrilesky 1995, 63). Bluntly put, "Arthur Burns experienced considerably more pressure to provide an expansive monetary policy" during the Carter administration than during the Ford administration (Havrilesky 1995, 64).

Ford's professional relationship with Burns was famous for the levels of congeniality and mutual respect that it evidenced. The relationship between Burns and Carter began on a sour note and apparently never recovered.[7] While Ford and Burns shared monetary policy preferences, macroeconomic objectives, and—not surprisingly—positions on the independence of the Fed,[8] Carter and Burns held none of these in common. From the beginning, Carter favored a more expansionary monetary policy, cared more about unemployment than about inflation, and expected greater Fed responsiveness to presidential pressure than Burns thought prudent. The conflict over the proper direction of monetary policy was so heated that during an oversight hearing on monetary policy, Senator Harrison Schmitt said to Burns,

> Unfortunately your appearance before the Banking Committee comes at a time of great conflict and confusion over monetary policy. . . . The conflict is between two directly opposing theories, one represented generally by you and the other by the President and his advisers. (*Senate Hearings* 1977, 3)

Evidence of the strained relations between Carter and Burns and of the frequency and virulence with which Carter and the members of his administration pressured Burns is not difficult to find. Burns's annoyance with Carter began even before the new president's election. Burns believed Carter's campaign rhetoric lacked proper respect for the independence of the Fed, and Burns disagreed with the thrust of Carter's macroeconomic policy proposals (Kettl 1986, 167). Kettl bluntly notes, "Relations between Carter and Burns got off to a bad start" (1986, 167). Over the course of the next year, relations between Burns and the Carter administration deteriorated. The conflict between Burns and the Carter administration was of such significance that Carter chose not to reappoint Burns at the end of his term as chairperson.

If Burns and the Fed had a poor relationship with the president during this time period, they were on better terms with Congress, at least by the end of Burns's tenure at the Fed in January 1978. Although the Fed was clearly in the congressional doghouse during the Ford administration, the attitudes of members of Congress mellowed by the end of 1977. During the Ford administration, the chairman of the Senate Banking Committee, William Proxmire, characterized the relationship between Fed policy and congressional policy objectives thus: "I think we can stress the differences, unfortunately, between your position, the Federal Reserve Board's position, and that of the Congress" (*Senate Hearings* 1976, 1). Henry Reuss, chairman of the House Banking Committee, feared that the Ford administration and the Fed were "ready to throw the economy into reverse, sacrificing jobs and production, at the first sighting of capacity bottlenecks or other isolated inflationary shoals" (*House Hearings* 1976, 2). These statements contrast markedly with Democratic Representative Frank Annunzio's 1978 pronouncement that

> as far as I am concerned inflation is not only our No.1 priority to be resolved, but it has reached a point of national emergency. . . . [W]hen you talk to the people, as far as they are concerned [inflation] is a national emergency. (*House Hearings* 1978, 135)

This quotation is clearly neither a ringing endorsement for the Carter administration's expansionary policy preferences nor a condemnation of the Fed's preference for tight-fisted monetary restraint.

As in the previous scenario, the multi-institutional model provides a theoretical framework for understanding the relationship between the actual policy chosen by the Fed and the policy preferences of the Fed, the president, and Congress. In this case, one can use the model to understand monetary policy-making during the early part of the Carter administration. Empirical evidence plainly indicates that the character of monetary policy changed between the latter part of the Ford administration and the early part of the Carter administration. According to Havrilesky, the Fed "initiated more rapid money supply growth in early 1977 in anticipation of the new Administration's realigned policy objectives" (1995, 63). Specifically, the yearly increase in M1 (a broad-based monetary aggregate) for 1977 was almost 1.5 percentage points higher than in 1976 (Degen 1987, 161), moving from 6.7 percent in 1976 to 8 percent in 1977.

Although Burns and other members of the Fed might not have been happy about the move to a more expansionary monetary policy, the political environment of the time offered them little choice. One can see why the political factors forced a change in policy at the Fed by studying figure 3.8.

P———O1———C———O2————————F   Fig. 3.8

Figure 3.8 is an exact duplicate of figure 3.7, with a single exception. The policy position of the president in figure 3.7 indicates a preference for a highly restrictive, anti-inflationary monetary policy; the policy position of the president in figure 3.8 indicates a preference for a very expansionary monetary policy. This corresponds to the change in presidential policy preferences from the inflation-fighting Ford to the expansion-minded Carter. With the change in presidential preferences, the Fed must ease up on monetary policy, moving actual policy to a position in line with C rather than O2.

This figure also provides an explanation for the contrast between the relationship between the Fed and Congress and the relationship between the Fed and Carter. With the election of Carter, the Fed was forced to change policy to coincide with Congress's ideal policy position. Not surprisingly, once this move was made, Congress was much more satisfied with the Fed's handling of monetary policy than it was during the Ford administration. Actual monetary policy is still, however, a considerable distance from the Carter ideal point. Even though monetary policy did ease in 1977, it is likely that the extent of this easing was unsatisfactory to the Carter administration.[9] Given this characterization of the situation, the continued rift between the Carter administration and the Fed is quite understandable.

The Later Carter Years—Breakdown of the Expansionary Consensus

The late Carter years (1979–80) witnessed a weakening of the congressional-presidential agreement on the direction of monetary policy. While Carter had the backing of a majority of senators and representatives for his expansionary objectives during at least the first year of his presidency, the midterm elections cut into this support. A loss of seats by the Democrats in both the House and the Senate allowed the Fed to rein in—to some extent—the economy during the last two years of Carter's presidency.

This situation demonstrates the impact of a shift in congressional preferences on policy even when the president, and arguably the president's preferences, remain the same. As Congress becomes more conservative, the Fed takes the opportunity to counteract an undesirably expansionist monetary policy from earlier years. In fact, the late Carter years are often taken as the most compelling anecdotal evidence against the proposition that the Fed eases monetary policy prior to an election (see Havrilesky and Gildea 1990). About this period in the Fed's history, Greider writes,

> If the Fed was trying to re-elect Carter, it went about it in a very strange way. . . . The close evidence, if anything, supported the opposite case—that the Federal Reserve was indifferent to Jimmy Carter's fate and quite willing to let monetary policy contribute to his defeat. (1987, 214)

Likewise, the "monetarist" experiment[10]—an FOMC policy change in the latter part of 1979—led to significantly lower increases in monetary aggregates and significantly higher interest rates.

Although Carter did change Fed chairpersons during the latter portion of his administration, the constriction in Fed policy cannot be solely attributed to the appointment of Paul Volcker. The contraction began prior to Volcker's appointment, as a quick comparison between interest rates in the first half of 1979 (pre-Volcker) and in the previous two years demonstrates. The average Fed Funds rate during the first half of 1979 was 10 percentage points. The yearly averages for both 1977 and 1978 were well below this figure (see Timberlake 1993). While the appointment of Volcker may have led to greater monetary tightness on the part of the Fed, the change in the political environment also played a role in the policy shift.

The Reagan Era—The Fed in Fine Shape

If the midterm elections in 1978 gave the Fed some maneuvering room for increasing interests rates and tightening monetary policy, Reagan's election and the Republican takeover in the Senate blew the doors off efforts to restrain Fed conservatism. With a president and Congress willing to turn the Fed loose to fight inflation—even if only for the short term—and a Fed chairperson able to take up the fight, the Fed moved to establish some of the most conservative monetary policy in recent memory. Not only did the Fed foster the highest nominal interest rates in decades, but it also generated some of the highest real rates in the twentieth century.

It was simply a time period in which the political environment was such that the Fed was free to pursue the contractionary policy it desired. Reagan's own early support for the Fed's conservative policy is difficult to doubt. Greider writes of Reagan's perspective,

> Ronald Reagan was as dedicated to restoring "sound money" as he was hostile to centralized government. Modern inflation, in fact, was an important particular in his indictment against Washington. . . . In order to break the raging price inflation, the President explained, money must be disciplined at its source—the central bank—and Reagan fully endorsed the Federal Reserve's commitment [to] slow down the growth of the money supply. (1987, 354)

Thus, presidential and congressional conservatism provided the foundation for the Fed's austerity program.

Conclusion

In this chapter I have introduced a multi-institutional model of monetary policy-making that integrates the institutional nature of the Fed's political environment with a treatment of the policy preferences of the elected political officials that might influence the Fed. This model provides provocative explanations for a number of significant, if not particularly well understood, empirical phenomena in the monetary policy-making arena, such as the relationship between presidential and congressional policy preferences and monetary policy. Using the Ford, Carter, and early Reagan years as case studies in monetary policy-making, I demonstrate how one can use the multi-institutional model to understand real-world policy-making phenomena.

The case studies presented here highlight the important aspects of the multi-institutional model. First, the preferences of the Fed's principals clearly have a significant impact on the actual policy chosen by the Fed. Second, given the institutional structure of the Fed's relationship with the houses of Congress and the president, the policy chosen by the Fed can often be quite far from the ideal policy of one or two of its principals (in a bicameral scenario). Third, the range of the Fed's independence—that is, the extent to which the Fed can achieve the price-stability objective—depends on the policy preferences of both the president and Congress. The level of Fed independence varies with shifts in the policy preferences of its principals, which clearly implies that formal institutions alone do not tell the whole story of Fed or, more generally, agency independence.

These cases also demonstrate the extent to which the Fed, as an agent, attempts to achieve its own policy objectives by using one or the other of its principals as a bulwark against the others. If the administration favors an expansionary policy, the Fed tends to move policy into line with the preferences of the more conservative house of Congress. If congressional preferences favor extreme expansion, the Fed tends to use the president's veto power—if the president is a Republican—as a shield against legislative reprisal.

This practice of playing one principal off against the other is not uncommon. Benjamin Strong, the most prominent central banker of the early twentieth century, once said, "In the face of a powerfully organized antagonism in Congress, the Federal Reserve System must, to a considerable extent, rely for its protection against political attack and interference upon the present administration" (quoted in Kane 1982, 232). Greider describes the gamesmanship of the Fed in the following terms: "[T]he central bank [the Fed] learned to frustrate the occasional challenges from either Congress or the executive branch by playing one off against the other" (1987, 279).

It is worth noting that the policy-making activities of bureaucracies, in general, were long ago characterized in this way. More than 40 years ago, Dahl and Lindblom wrote, "Bureaucratic leaders are participants in a bargaining process. If their status, power, or security is threatened by Presidential politicians, they stimulate an alliance with Congressional politicians. Conversely, if menaced by Congressional politicians, they look to the Presidential politicians for allies" (1953, 342–43). While the recent (or multi-institutional) treatments of bureaucratic policy-making have hinted at this dynamic, its existence had not yet been demonstrated in a particular policy-making environment. Clearly, this dynamic is at work in the politics of monetary policy-making, as it probably is in other specific policy arenas.

The basic multi-institutional model clearly generates empirically testable implications. However, it might be argued that these implications are very sensitive to model specification. What would happen if one relaxed the assumption dealing with the constancy and conservatism of Fed policy preferences? Or what if members of Congress incurred costs for taking action against the Fed, regardless of the president's reaction? Would the relationships specified in the basic model presented in this chapter manifest themselves in a less restrictive model? I address these questions in the next chapter.

CHAPTER 4

The Multi-Institutional Model, Part 2: Relaxing Assumptions on the Way to a General Model

The basic multi-institutional model presented in chapter 3 is based on at least two fairly restrictive simplifying assumptions:

1. Fed policy preferences are (a) constant and (b) consistent with price stability to the point that they are at least as conservative as the preferences of the most conservative override voter in Congress, and
2. congressional actions are costless unless they are overturned.

Although the Fed is usually characterized as being a fairly conservative, nonexpansionary institution, such might not always be the case. In some situations, the Fed might conceivably have more expansionary policy preferences than the president and many members of Congress. Likewise, significant shifts or changes in Fed preferences are not impossible.

By the same token, members of Congress may not be completely free to act in a way that is consistent with their policy preferences. For example, if Fed officials—or their political associates or supporters—sense that an acute constraint has been placed on the Fed's conduct of monetary policy, they may attempt to lobby members of Congress in such a way that would increase the costs associated with taking action the Fed would find unpleasant and undesirable. If this phenomenon occurs, and congressional activity becomes costly, then it is not clear that anything like the implications of the basic multi-institutional model would still hold. To evaluate the impact of this change in assumptions it is necessary to examine a version of the multi-institutional model in which these assumptions are relaxed.

When Federal Reserve Preferences Change

Previously, I have assumed that the Fed's policy preferences are constant; by assumption, the Fed always favors that policy position which is consistent with price stability.[1] Therefore, in the original model, deviations from a policy consistent with price stability were attributed to credible threats of legislative sanction.

While some scholars assume that the Fed's policy preferences are always consistent with the price-stability objective (see Cukierman 1992), it is quite likely that Fed preferences vary. The empirical evidence indicates that the individual policy preferences of Fed governors vary widely (see Chappell, Havrilesky, and McGregor 1990; Havrilesky 1995; Havrilesky and Gildea 1990; Gildea 1990). Realizing that the membership of the Board of Governors and FOMC change periodically as governors and bank presidents come and go, one would also expect the aggregate policy preference of the body to change over time. If the president and the Senate attempt to use their powers of appointment and confirmation to mold the Fed's policy preferences through the manipulation of personnel, it is all the more reason to think that Fed policy preferences vary over time.

The appointment power is widely regarded as an important means by which presidents influence the policy preferences of members of the Board of Governors.[2] A number of prominent students of monetary policy-making identify the appointment power as one of the most useful tools available to the president for modifying the Fed's policy preferences. Chappell, Havrilesky, and McGregor make perhaps the strongest statement of the importance of the appointment power for molding the Fed's policy preferences; they contend that "the appointments process is the primary mechanism by which partisan differences in monetary policy arise" (1993, 185). The appointment power is an important means of influencing monetary policy-making to the extent that it can be used to alter "the values and theoretical outlooks of Federal Reserve Board members" (Woolley 1984, 115). If appointee choice has an impact on the policy preferences of the Fed—as one might logically assume—then the assumption that the Fed always prefers a particular monetary policy position (i.e., a policy consistent with price stability) appears inappropriately restrictive.

If one assumes that the president (through the appointment power) and the Senate (through the confirmation prerogative) have the capacity to manipulate the Fed's policy preferences, then it is useful to know how this manipulation affects actual monetary policy. In chapter 5, I investigate the president's use of the appointment power and the Senate's use of the confirmation prerogative. I also assess the extent to which the president and the Senate can actually modify the Fed's policy preferences through the appointment and confirmation of Fed governors.

Whether the president and the Senate effectively manipulate Fed preferences, it is quite likely that Fed policy preferences vary. Thus, it is necessary to understand the relationship between variations in Fed preferences and variations in actual policy. It is also important to attempt to understand the impact of congressional threats and presidential protection on monetary policy in an environment where Fed preferences are variable.

I am specifically interested in answering the following questions:

1. If Fed preferences vary, what is the relationship between the Fed's ideal and actual policies?
2. Also, if Fed policy preferences vary, do changes in congressional and presidential preferences have the same impact on monetary policy as they do in the original model presented in chapter 3?

At first glance, the answers to these questions might seem obvious. One would intuitively assume that shifts in Fed policy preferences would be reflected in corresponding shifts in actual policy. However, the case study analysis presented in the previous chapter demonstrates that the Fed does not always get what it wants. In fact, the results from chapter 3 indicate that the Fed rarely, if ever, gets to choose the exact policy that it deems most desirable. Thus, in a policy-making environment in which choice is restricted, it is not at all clear that shifts in the Fed's policy preferences automatically generate corresponding movements in policy.

It is easy to construct a scenario that demonstrates that a change in the Fed's policy preferences does not result in a corresponding change in policy. Take, for instance, the scenario depicted in figure 4.1 (which reverts to the original unicameral-legislature model for ease of exposition):

————O1————C————O2-F1——F2,P   Fig. 4.1

If the Fed's ideal policy position is represented by F1, then the Fed will have to choose position O2 as the actual policy position. A choice of any position closer to F1 would result in a veto-proof legislative sanction of the Fed. Now consider the result of a change in the Fed's ideal policy position. If the Fed's ideal policy position moves from F1 to F2, the actual policy position remains the same, O2. Choosing a position closer to F2 than O2 would again result in a veto-proof legislative sanction.

Of course, this result does not always obtain. The more intuitive result—the one where a shift in the Fed's policy preferences does generate a corresponding movement in actual policy—can also occur within the structure of this model, as figure 4.2 illustrates.

————O1————C-F2——O2————F1,P   Fig. 4.2

In this scenario, the ideal policy position of the Fed moves from point F1 to point F2. This shift in the Fed's policy preferences—unlike the shift in figure 4.1—generates a corresponding change in the policy position chosen by the Fed. Actual policy shifts from O2 to F2. The Fed need not choose a policy position other than F2 since the threat of a presidential veto protects it from sanction.

These short examples offer at least two insights into the relationship between changes in the ideal policy preferences of the Fed and changes in the actual policy chosen by the Fed:

1. For certain congressional, presidential, and Fed preference distributions, variations in the Fed's policy preferences result in corresponding changes in actual policy position—that is, a move toward greater monetary restraint (ease) in the Fed's ideal policy position results in a move toward greater restraint (ease) in the actual policy chosen.
2. For certain other congressional, presidential, and Fed preference distributions, variations in the Fed's policy preferences result in no change in the actual policy position chosen—that is, a move toward greater monetary restraint (ease) in the ideal policy position of the Fed has no effect on the actual policy position chosen.

Before trying to identify in greater detail the specific impact of shifts in the Fed's policy preferences on the actual policy chosen by the Fed, it is important to identify the potential actual policy positions that the Fed will choose if its policy preferences vary across the policy space.

Consider figure 4.3:

—SO1——HO1—S—H——SO2—HO2——P—   Fig. 4.3

What would the Fed choose as the actual policy position if congressional and presidential policy preferences were distributed in this manner and the Fed's ideal policy position were between HO2 and P? What if the Fed's ideal policy position were between H and SO2? Or between HO1 and S? Given the distribution of policy preferences in figure 4.3, the relationship between the Fed's ideal and actual policy positions can be described as follows, with F_i indicating the Fed's ideal policy position and F_a indicating the Fed's actual policy choice:[3]

1. If $HO2 \leq F_i \leq P$, then F_a will be HO2. If the Fed chooses any point to the right of HO2, it is subject to a veto-proof sanction.
2. If $S \leq F_i < HO2$, then $F_a = F_i$. The presidential veto protects the Fed from sanction if $S \leq F_a < HO2$. If $S \leq F_a \leq H$, then the House and the Senate will not jointly favor any single point to F_a and veto protection is unnecessary; thus, the Fed will not be sanctioned.

3. If $F_i < S$, then $F_a = S$. If the Fed chooses any point $< S$, it is subject to sanction.

When attempting to discern the relationship between the Fed's ideal and actual policy positions, one should keep three characteristics of the model in mind. First, the Fed will never incite a sanction. Second, Congress will only sanction the Fed if there is no credible threat of a presidential veto. Third, Congress will only sanction the Fed if there is some actual policy position that both the House and the Senate prefer to the one chosen by the Fed. With an understanding of these aspects of the model, it is not difficult to comprehend the relationship between F_i and F_a in the previous scenarios.

Suppose the president's ideal policy position is at the opposite boundary of the policy space, at the left end of the line in figure 4.3. How does this change affect the relationship between F_i and F_a? Not surprisingly, the results associated with this second scenario are a mirror image of those for the scenario depicted in figure 4.3. Figure 4.4 depicts the new scenario:

P—SO1——HO1—S—H——SO2—HO2   Fig. 4.4

One can describe the results as follows:

1. If $P \leq F_i \leq SO1$, then the Fed will choose as F_a point SO1. If the Fed chooses any point to the left of SO1, it is subject to a veto-proof sanction.
2 If $SO1 \leq F_i < H$, then $F_a = F_i$. The presidential veto protects the Fed from sanction if $SO1 \leq F_a < S$. If $S \leq F_a < H$, then the House and the Senate will not jointly favor any single point to F_a; thus, the Fed will not be sanctioned.
3. If $F_i > H$, then $F_a = H$. If the Fed chooses any point $> H$, it is subject to sanction.

Notice how S's replace H's (and SO1's replace HO2's) when one moves from the implications of the first scenario to the implications of the second. This change illustrates the mirror-image relationship between the scenarios.

Now that there is a sense of the relationship between the Fed's ideal policy position and the actual policy position chosen in these two static scenarios, I will next consider the dynamic relationship between F_i and F_a in these two scenarios. To begin, one can see that the potential area of points from which the Fed can choose an actual policy position is bounded by the override point nearest the president's ideal policy position and the ideal policy position of the house furthest from the president. The Fed will not choose any F_a point beyond these points. The Fed clearly will never choose any policy point that is outside either of the most extreme override boundaries. To do so would result in a veto-proof congressional sanction of Fed policy. The Fed will also avoid policy positions that are more extreme than the ideal policy position of the chamber furthest from the president, because the president will be unwilling to protect the Fed with a veto of congressional sanction under those circumstances.

Another result that can be given up front is the exact correspondence of the Fed's policy preferences and actual policy when $S \leq F_i \leq H$. As long as the Fed's ideal policy position is not outside the space bounded by the ideal policy positions of both houses of Congress, the Fed can and will choose the policy that exactly corresponds to its own preferences. It is readily apparent that no point in the interval [S,H] is preferred by both chambers simultaneously to any other point in that interval. Thus, regardless of the Fed's position, as long as its policy choice is within that interval, it will avoid sanction.

Given these results and those from the two static scenarios, it should not be difficult to see that, regardless of the movement of the Fed's ideal policy position, actual policy will never move in a contrary manner. In no region of the policy space is there an inverse relationship between movements in the Fed's policy preferences and actual policy. While there are regions in the policy space where shifts in the Fed's ideal point have no impact on actual policy (i.e., when the Fed's ideal point varies in a region beyond the override points), a movement in the Fed's policy preferences will never result in a movement of actual policy in the opposite direction.

In sum, the revised multi-institutional model presented in this section has the following implications:

1. If the Fed's ideal and actual policy positions covary, they are directly (i.e., positively) related. Assuming the covariance of these two variables, if the Fed's preferences move toward greater tightness, actual monetary policy will follow.
2. However, in certain regions of the policy space, the Fed's ideal policy position and the actual policy position chosen by the Fed do not covary. Sometimes a change in Fed policy preferences will have no impact on actual policy.

These results should clarify the relationship between the Fed's policy preferences and actual monetary policy in a policy-making environment in which presidential and congressional preferences are constant. I now move on to an investigation of the relationship between the policy preferences of the Fed, the Congress, and the president and actual monetary policy when Fed, congressional, and presidential policy preferences all vary.

The Impact of Congressional and Presidential Policy Preferences on Monetary Policy When All Preferences May Vary

Realizing that the relationship between the Fed's policy preferences and actual policy is not always what one might intuitively expect, it is reasonable to doubt that variations in congressional and presidential policy preferences have the impact on monetary policy indicated in the previous chapter. If Fed policy preferences vary, are there some circumstances under which shifts in congressional preferences have no impact on monetary policy? Are there circumstances under which variations in presidential preferences have no impact on monetary policy? These questions remain unanswered.

The analysis presented in the previous chapter generated several specific results pertaining to the relationship between variations in presidential and congressional policy preferences and variations in monetary policy. Assuming that the House is the more conservative chamber, the implications of the original model were as follows:

1. The Fed's actual policy positions will reflect the president's monetary policy preferences. Monetary policy will tighten (loosen) as presidential policy preferences become more restrictive (less restrictive), ceteris paribus.
2. The Fed's actual policy positions will reflect the House's monetary policy preferences. Monetary policy will tighten (loosen) as House policy preferences become more restrictive (less restrictive), ceteris paribus.
3. The Fed's actual policy positions will not reflect the Senate's monetary policy preferences.

I now move to an evaluation of the extent to which these results are also implications of the revised model, in which Fed policy preferences are allowed to vary across the range of the policy space.

To begin, how does presidential influence—as exercised through the veto threat—affect monetary policy-making in the revised model? In general, the relationship between shifts in presidential policy preferences and movements in actual policy is similar to that relationship in the original model. For example, consider the scenario presented in figures 4.5 and 4.6.

——SO1——HO1—S——H——SO2-F_i-HO2————P   Fig. 4.5

P—SO1——HO1—S——H——SO2-F_i-HO2————   Fig. 4.6

If the president's ideal policy position is the right boundary of the policy space, the Fed can choose a policy that exactly corresponds with its own preferences. However, if the president's policy preferences move to the left boundary of the policy space, the Fed must choose a policy no farther to the right than H to avoid legislative sanction. Although the Fed's ideal policy position has moved from the right boundary of the policy space, the change in presidential preferences reflecting a desire for greater monetary ease has resulted in a movement of actual policy to a position of greater monetary ease.

In general, the relationship between movements in presidential preferences and monetary policy identified in chapter 3 still holds when the Fed's preferences are allowed to vary across the spectrum of the policy space.[4] The only situation for which this relationship does not hold is when the Fed's preferences lie between those of the House and Senate, as figure 4.7 shows.

——SO1——HO1—S-F_i-H——SO2——HO2————   Fig. 4.7

Regardless of the president's position, the Fed can choose its optimal monetary policy without fear of legislative sanction. Since the House and Senate do not jointly prefer any point to F_i, the Fed will not be sanctioned.

I will now turn to the relationship between shifts in congressional policy preferences and actual policy in a world of varying Fed policy preferences. As before, it is important to distinguish between Senate policy preferences and those of the House. In an important respect, those results should not be associated with the revised model. In the theoretical world characterized by the revised model, the impact of shifts in House preferences and in Senate preferences depends specifically on the Fed's own policy preferences. If, as I have assumed from the beginning, the House prefers a tighter monetary policy than does the Senate, shifts in the House's preferences will only have an impact on monetary policy as long as the Fed prefers a tighter policy than does the House. Conversely, while the Senate's policy preferences had no impact on monetary policy in the world of the original model, they can affect monetary policy in the revised model. More specifically, the policy preferences of the more expansionist-minded chamber can have an impact on monetary policy if the Fed prefers a more liberal or expansionary monetary policy than that desired by that chamber. To help with the intuition behind these results, I offer several related examples.

Suppose the Fed favors a more restrictive monetary policy than does the House (and, by assumption, the Senate). One way to characterize the distribution of preferences would be as in figure 4.8:

$$P\text{—}SO1\text{——}HO1\text{—}S\text{—}H\text{——}SO2\text{-}F_i\text{-}HO2\text{——}$$

Fig. 4.8

In figure 4.8, the Fed's choice of monetary policy is clearly effectively constrained by the House's policy preferences. The Fed cannot choose a tighter monetary policy than that which corresponds to the House's ideal policy position with subjecting itself to sanction. The influence of House policy preferences in this scenario does not depend on the president's position, as figure 4.8A shows:

$$\text{——}SO1\text{——}HO1\text{—}S\text{—}H\text{——}SO2\text{-}F_i\text{-}HO2\text{——}P$$

Fig. 4.8A

In this scenario, the president's position has moved from the left side of the policy space to the right side. Nevertheless, the Fed's choice of policy still depends on House preferences (in this case, the position of the House override point HO2). If the House's policy preferences shift to the left or right, actual policy will follow. As in the original version of the model, variations in Senate preferences have no impact on monetary policy-making.[5]

Suppose, however, that the Fed's policy preferences are far more expansionary than previously assumed. Imagine that the Fed prefers a policy somewhere between the House's ideal point and the House's left override point. If this is the case, figure 4.9 is one way to characterize the situation:

$$\text{——}SO1\text{——}HO1\text{—}F_i\text{—}S\text{—}H\text{—}SO2\text{—}HO2\text{——}P$$

Fig. 4.9

If the Fed's ideal policy position is at F_i, then it will choose as the actual policy position a policy that exactly corresponds to the preferences of the Senate, not the House. A shift in the Senate's preferences would lead to a corresponding shift in monetary policy.[6] In this scenario, House preferences and their shifts have no impact on monetary policy.

Finally, it is possible for the Fed's policy preferences to be such that shifts in the preferences of either house of Congress have no impact on the position of actual policy. Consider the scenario in figure 4.10.

$$\text{——}SO1\text{——}HO1\text{—}S\text{—}F_i\text{—}H\text{—}SO2\text{—}HO2\text{——}P$$

Fig. 4.10

As noted previously, when the Fed prefers a policy that is somewhere between the policy preferred by the Senate and that preferred by the

House, the Fed can choose an actual policy that exactly corresponds with its own preferences. This scenario also holds true for a model in which congressional policy preferences are allowed to vary. Regardless of the shifts in Senate and House preferences—and regardless of the shifts in presidential policy preferences—the Fed can always choose its own ideal policy as the actual policy as long as the ideal lies in the region of the policy space bounded by the ideal policy positions of the House and Senate.

In general, shifts in congressional and presidential policy preferences generate corresponding shifts in actual monetary policy if they generate movement in policy at all. The specific results for all scenarios are summarized in table 4.1.[7] Two things should be kept in mind while examining the results in table 4.1:

1. By assumption, the Senate has more expansionary policy preferences than does the House.
2. The relationship between a particular house's ideal policy position and its override points is constant. Thus, a shift in the ideal policy position implies a corresponding shift in the override points.

When Congressional Actions Are Costly

Until now, I have assumed that policy actions are costless unless they are overturned, in which case the costs are prohibitive. Thus, members of Congress face no costs associated with passing a sanction of the Fed unless the president issues an override-proof veto of that legislation. What would happen if the members of Congress incurred a cost simply by passing legislation (regardless of the president's reaction) or overriding a veto? Would the implications of the multi-institutional model be altered by either of these extensions/generalizations?

The short answers are as follows:

1. Ceteris paribus, there will be an inverse relationship between costs and the distance in the policy space between the Fed's ideal policy position and actual policy.
2. As long as the costs of congressional action are not prohibitive, the incorporation of costs has no impact on the basic implications of the multi-institutional model.

The remainder of this section explains and develops these results.

To incorporate costs into the multi-institutional model, it is necessary to find some way to designate these costs in the current metric of disutility—distance in the policy space. One way to do so is to designate or specify a preferential equivalency for members of Congress—those actors fac-

TABLE 4.1. Monetary Policy and the Effect of Shifts in Presidential and Congressional Preferences when Fed Preferences Vary

Scenario	Fed Response To:		
	Shift in Presidential Preferences	Shift in Senate Preferences[a]	Shift in House Preferences
P < SO1 < HO1 < S < H < SO2 < HO2 < F	Corresponding shift in policy	No policy change	Corresponding shift in policy
P < SO1 < HO1 < S < H < SO2 < F ≤ HO2	Corresponding shift in policy	No policy change	Corresponding shift in policy
P < SO1 < HO1 < S < H < F ≤ SO2 < HO2	Corresponding shift in policy	No policy change	Corresponding shift in policy
P < SO1 < HO1 < S < F ≤ H < SO2 < HO2	No policy change	No policy change	Corresponding shift in policy
P < SO1 < HO1 < F ≤ S < H < SO2 < SO2	Corresponding shift in policy or no policy change (i.e., if F = H)	No policy change	No policy change
P < SO1 < F ≤ HO1 < S < H < SO2 < HO2	Corresponding shift in policy	No policy change	No Policy change
P < F ≤ SO1 < HO1 < S < H < SO2 < HO2	Corresponding shift in policy	Corresponding shift in policy	No policy change
F ≤ P < SO1 < HO1 < S < H < SO2 < HO2	Corresponding shift in policy	Corresponding shift in policy	No policy change

[a] I assume that the shift in chamber preferences is not large enough to change the ordering of congressional preferences (i.e., the more conservative house prior to a shift is also the more conservative house after the shift).

ing the costs of action—between a monetary policy, x, chosen by the Fed (i.e., without the need for congressional sanction and the incurred costs) and monetary policy, y, established by Congress through Fed sanction (thus forcing Congress to incur the costs of congressional action). If the costs are nontrivial, then dx + costs = dy (where d is the distance operator) for all members in the unicameral version of the model. So, in the case of the median voter, when x corresponds to C and y corresponds to C_{cl} (cl referring to costs-left), then $dC + costs = dC_{cl}$.

How will the imposition of costs—or the assumption of costly congressional action—influence the depiction of the multi-institutional model? The only change is that indifference points will need to be identified. The imposition of costs should generate indifference points on both sides of the ideal point for each member of Congress. The most important indifference points will be those for the override voters and the median voter. More specifically, it should be obvious that, for all practical purposes, the only indifference points that matter are those that fall between the override and median voter positions, individually, and the Fed's ideal policy position. So, in a unicameral world, the imposition of costs would be diagrammatically illustrated as in figure 4.11.

$$-O1_{cl}-O1-O1_{cr}-C_{cl}-C-C_{cr}-O2_{cl}-O2-O2_{cr}----P,F$$ Fig. 4.11

In figure 4.11, the override voter with an ideal policy position at O1 is indifferent between O1 and $O1_{cl}$ and $O1_{cr}$ if costs must be incurred— action must be taken—to achieve O1 and the achievement of $O1_{cl}$ or $O1_{cr}$ is costless. If the Fed chooses some policy x, and $O2 < x < O2_{cr}$, the override voter will not support punishment of the Fed to achieve O2 because the voter prefers x (sans costs) to O2 with costs. This dynamic illustrates something quite important. The most significant difference between the basic multi-institutional model and the model that incorporates costly congressional action is that actual policy is likely to be closer to the Fed's ideal policy in the costly action model. In fact, the following implication is easily proven:

> Ceteris paribus, the actual monetary policy chosen will never be farther from the Fed's ideal policy in the multi-institutional model with costly action than in the model with costless actions. There are, however, situations in which an increase in the costs of congressional action will have no impact on Fed policy-making.

That the Fed can choose a policy closer to its own ideal point in an environment in which Congress must pay a price for its actions is obvious.

But the fact that the imposition of costs will, in some circumstances, have no impact on policy is less intuitive. Consider, for a moment, the situation in which the Fed's ideal policy preferences lie between those of the median voter in the House and the median voter in the Senate. Under these circumstances in a costless environment, the Fed can choose its own ideal policy as the actual policy. The same is true in a world in which Congress incurs costs due to sanctioning efforts. Thus, in this situation the imposition of costs has no impact on the character of monetary policy.

Although the Fed's newfound freedom can be substantial—depending on Fed preferences, congressional preferences, and the costliness of action—there is a similarity between the basic (costless) multi-institutional model and the less restrictive model. The imposition of costs associated with congressional action—assuming they are not prohibitive[8]—does no damage to the relationships between shifts in congressional policy preferences and actual monetary policy identified in the basic multi-institutional model.

Even in a costly environment, the Fed must still be sensitive to changes in the policy preferences of members of Congress and the president. To see this dynamic at work, consider the policy scenario illustrated in figure 4.12:

$$\text{———}O1_{cr}\text{———}C_{cl}\text{———}O2_{cr}\text{———}P,F \qquad\qquad \text{Fig. 4.12}$$

Figure 4.12 is simply a copy of figure 4.11 with the original median and override points deleted and the expansionist side median and override voter points deleted. For the Fed's strategic purposes, these points are irrelevant. On this realization, the pared-down figure resembles in every detail the very first illustrations of the basic unicameral multi-institutional model. Just as in that environment, the Fed chooses a policy position equivalent to the ideal policy position of the most conservative override voter (O2); in this environment the Fed chooses a policy position that is equivalent to the ideal policy position of that same voter plus costs. The figure above can also be used to illustrate an equally important similarity between the basic multi-institutional model and the new, costly model. If the costs are constant, as I assume, a change in the policy preferences of Congress or the president will result in a change in Fed policy that would be equivalent to the change in a costless policy-making environment. For any given change in preferences, though the starting and ending points may be closer to the Fed's ideal, in the costly environment as opposed to the costless environment the distance between the starting and ending points will be exactly the same. Therefore, even in an environment in which Congress incurs costs for sanctioning the Fed, the Fed will still be sensitive to congressional and presidential policy preferences, assuming costs are not prohibitive.

A Note on Political Activity at the Federal Reserve

Suppose that the Fed is more than a political player reacting to the changes in the policy preferences of members of Congress and the president. Let us also suppose that members of the Board of Governors and the FOMC have political clout of their own and/or have personal and professional contacts who have political clout. If the governors, reserve bank presidents, and their contacts mobilized to achieve their policy goals, one focal point might be generating costs associated with congressional action.[9] Treatments of the politics of monetary policy-making, particularly the more journalistic approaches, often argue that the Fed uses its political muscle to influence congressional activities in the monetary policy arena.

While some may argue that the Fed and its allies lobby Congress in an effort to change the policy preferences of members, the more likely lobbying objective is to make political action—particularly sanctions—more costly to members of Congress. Even if the Fed effectively participates in this type of political activity, the exposition in this chapter indicates that the Fed must still be responsive to shifts in congressional and presidential policy preferences.

Conclusions

In this chapter, I have extended the generality of the basic multi-institutional model by relaxing two of the most important original assumptions: (1) the assumption that Fed policy preferences are constant and conservative, and (2) the assumption that Congress incurs no costs when it invokes sanctions. I demonstrate that the implications of the basic multi-institutional model are, for the most part, still true of the more general model. Explicitly, under most policy-making conditions, the Fed must still be sensitive to and respond to changes in the policy preferences of members of Congress and the president.

Nevertheless, the Fed's own policy preferences also clearly have an important impact on policy. Although I have assumed, up to this point, that the president's capacity to influence policy is a function of the veto power, the president might also influence policy through the use of the appointment power. In fact, if presidents can manipulate Fed policy preferences with the appointment power, then the multi-institutional model may grossly underestimate the strength of the relationship between presidential policy preferences and actual policy. The next chapter will consider the role of the president's appointment power in the monetary policy-making arena.

CHAPTER 5

The Appointment Process at the Federal Reserve: Does the President Dominate? Does It Matter?

It is clear from the multi-institutional analysis presented in chapter 4 that shifts in the Fed's policy preferences can have an impact on the character of monetary policy. During a Democratic administration, if the Fed prefers a more expansionary policy than does the median voter in the most conservative house, then policy will be more expansionary than if the Fed preferred a more restrictive policy. During a Republican administration, if the Fed prefers a more expansionary policy than that preferred by the legislator at the most conservative override point, then policy will be more expansionary than if the Fed preferred a more restrictive policy. The policy that the Fed actually wants will obviously have an impact on the way in which it reacts to the constraints it faces. Likewise, the analysis in the preceding chapter suggests that the extent to which shifts in Fed preferences are reflected in policy depends on the political context in which the shift occurs (i.e., the preferences of the other actors).

Fed policy preferences are a function of the individual policy preferences of the members of the Board of Governors and the FOMC.[1] Since appointees' policy preferences have an impact on Fed policy-making, one wonders what factors influence the president's choice of nominee and the Senate's confirmation decision. Traditionally, scholars assumed that the type of appointee chosen depended on the president's policy preferences alone. Woolley's description of the means available to Congress for influencing Fed policy-making completely ignores the confirmation prerogative (1984, 132–33). When Chappell, Havrilesky, and McGregor (1990) attempt to estimate the ideal interest-rate preferences for individual Fed appointees, they omit any consideration of the impact of Senate policy preferences on these individual interest-rate preferences. Finally, Havrilesky and Gildea's (1990) explanation for the appointment of "unreliable" governors does not include the potentially restrictive impact of Senate policy preferences on the president's choice of nominee.

Current work on the appointment process suggests that the policy preferences of both the Senate and the president influence the type of individual nominated and confirmed for a position in an administrative or regulatory agency. In a formal analysis of the nomination and confirmation process, Hammond and Hill write, "Our basic conclusion is that both the Senate and the president have a fundamental role in the politics of appointments" (1993, 57). Hammond and Hill go on to emphasize the complex, interactive nature of the roles of the Senate and the president in the nomination and confirmation process, contending that the

> evidence that most nominees are confirmed does not show that the [sic] either the President or the Senate dominates appointment politics. Our analysis shows that the issue is more complicated. Empirical analysis must be structured so as to reflect this complexity, looking less at the influence of the Senate or of the President, and instead examining the conditions in which their relative influence may vary. (1993, 57)

A recent formal analysis of the Fed nomination and confirmation process also suggests that the Senate plays an important role. Results from Waller's (1992) model of the appointment process imply that reliable appointees—who consistently support the partisan policies of the nominating presidents—are much less likely to be nominated and confirmed during periods of divided government (i.e., White House and Senate controlled by opposing parties) than during periods of united government (i.e., White House and Senate controlled by the same party). In an attempt to understand the complex interrelationship between the Senate and the president, particularly during periods of divided government, Waller focuses on the timing of Fed appointments.

The results of his bargaining model indicate that the more distant the next presidential election, the greater the president's bargaining leverage with the Senate; thus, during periods of divided government, appointments made early in a president's term face less partisan opposition than those made near the end of the term. According to Waller,

> The intuition behind this result follows from the fact that the out-of-power party has an incentive to reject nominations to the board since, if it wins the next election, it will get to appoint someone to fill the vacancy who is more to its liking. (1992, 413)

Thus, during periods of divided government, the nearer the next presidential election, the more we should expect to see the Senate restrict the president's choice of nominees. Empirical analyses presented by Havrilesky

(1995) and Chappell, Havrilesky, and McGregor (1993) provide some support for these conjectures.

In this chapter, I discuss several facets of the Fed appointment process, and I integrate the appointment process into the multi-institutional model developed in previous chapters. First, I present some descriptive and historical analyses that suggest that presidents face at least three obstacles when they attempt to use the appointment power to influence Fed policy-making. These obstacles are:

1. The number of appointment opportunities for any particular president is limited.
2. Appointees may be unreliable (the Earl Warren effect).[2]
3. If the Senate's policy preferences diverge from those of the president, the president's appointee choice set is restricted.

The first obstacle might be overcome if it could be demonstrated that the Fed chairperson's preferences dominate policy-making. In that case, the president would need only to appoint the chairperson to control Fed policy-making. I evaluate the claim that the president's main tool for manipulation of the Fed is via the power to appoint the chair. I discuss the implications of these considerations for the president's capacity to affect monetary policy by modifying the Fed's policy preferences through the appointment process. I conclude by suggesting that the multi-institutional nature of Fed policy-making—and the multiagent character of the Fed's main policy-making body, the FOMC—limits the president's capacity to influence monetary policy via the appointment process.

Nominations, Confirmations, and the Federal Reserve: Opportunities and Constraints

Since the 1951 accord—the agreement between the Fed and the Treasury department that is widely cited as the beginning of Fed independence (see Woolley 1984 and Havrilesky 1995)—every president except Eisenhower and Kennedy has appointed more than the institutionally insured average of two governors per electoral term (see table 5.1). Presidents often have the opportunity to appoint more governors than the institutional structure of the Fed would lead one to expect because governors customarily retire before their terms end. While governors M. S. Szymczak (1933–61) and J .L. Robertson (1952–73) served for decades, many governors serve less than five years. G. William Miller (1978–79) and David Lilly (1976–78) each served less than two years. In general, very few governors serve complete fourteen-year terms.

Nevertheless, presidents still find it difficult to "pack" the board. Table 5.2 gives some indication of the amount of time recent presidents have enjoyed a Board of Governors packed with enough of their appointees to control—by majority vote—the FOMC.[3]

As the data presented in table 5.2 show, presidents regularly spend significant portions of their administrations without a single appointee on the Board of Governors. On average, more than 75 percent of a president's term in office is spent before the opportunity to appoint a majority of the

TABLE 5.1.   Presidents and Seats Filled on the Board of Governors, 1953–1996

Eisenhower	3
Kennedy	2
Johnson	4
Nixon	5
Ford	5
Carter	5
Reagan	7
Bush	3
Clinton	4

Note: Individual presidents are given credit for one appointment per seat. Eisenhower, Carter, and Reagan all made double appointments to single seats. When presidents reappoint appointees of previous presidents, the reappointing president gets credit for the governor at the point of reappointment.

TABLE 5.2.   Number of Months Each President Had Own Appointees in 0, 1–3, 4–6, or 7 Seats on the Board of Governors (not including appointees of fellow partisans)

President[a]	0 seats	1–3 seats	4–6 seats	7 seats
Eisenhower (96)	18	78	0	0
Kennedy (21)	7	14	0	0
Johnson (75)	2	52	21	0
Nixon (66)	12	40	14	0
Ford (30)	3	15	12	0
Carter (48)	13	16	19	0
Reagan (96)	13	47	31	5
Bush (48)	15	33	0	0
Clinton (48)	20	22	6	0
Average	11.4	35.2	11.4	0.6

[a]The number in parentheses following each president's name is the number of months that president served in office.

TABLE 5.3. Number of Months Each President Had Own Appointees or
Fellow Partisan Appointees in 0, 1–3, 4–6, or 7 Seats on the Board of Governors

President[a]	0 seats	1–3 seats	4–6 seats	7 seats
Eisenhower (96)	18	78	0	0
Kennedy (21)	0	0	21	0
Johnson (75)	0	0	75	0
Nixon (66)	12	40	14	0
Ford (30)	0	5	17	8
Carter (48)	13	16	19	0
Reagan (96)	0	36	42	18
Bush (48)	0	0	0	48
Clinton (48)	20	22	6	0
Average	7.0	21.9	21.6	8.2

[a]The number in parentheses following each president's name is the number of months that
president served in office. See Chappell, Havrilesky, and McGregor 1993.

Board of Governors arises. On a related note, presidents almost never
make sufficient appointments to control the FOMC via majority vote.
Even if a president is fortunate enough to have control of each of the seven
seats on the FOMC, this opportunity comes only in the waning moments
of a presidency.

Even taking into account the support presidents might receive from
the appointees of fellow partisans, the appointment power is not a particularly effective means of gaining control of the Fed. First, many presidents
do not succeed fellow partisans. From 1953 to 1996 the United States had
nine presidents, only three of whom—Lyndon Johnson, Gerald Ford, and
George Bush—followed fellow partisans. Second, even after including
appointments of fellow partisans, presidents still spend significant portions of their administrations with few supporters on the FOMC (see table
5.3). Even when counting the appointees of fellow partisans, presidents
usually serve more than half their first terms before the opportunity to
appoint a majority of the Board of Governors arises. Thus, it seems that
opportunities to pack the board and the FOMC are truly rare.

The Problem of Appointee Reliability

The preceding tables almost certainly overestimate the impact of the president's appointment power on policy-making at the Fed. As noted previously, presidents rarely have the opportunity to pack the Board of Governors. When they are able to do so, it is only near the ends of their
administrations, and recent research indicates that electoral and legislative

pressures prevent presidents near the ends of their terms from appointing reliable governors to the Fed (Havrilesky and Gildea 1990; Havrilesky 1995; Waller 1992). Economists appointed to the board support the policy positions of their appointing presidents far more reliably than do noneconomist appointees (Havrilesky and Gildea 1990; Havrilesky 1995), and presidents tend to appoint economists early in their terms and noneconomists late in their terms (Havrilesky and Gildea 1990; Havrilesky 1995). Havrilesky and Gildea (1990) provide an electorally motivated explanation for this phenomenon: "[N]oneconomists tend to be elite leaders from private banking and industry. As such they can generate far more political support in the form of campaign resources for the appointing President than can decidedly more pedestrian, technocratic economists" (Havrilesky and Gildea 1990, 54).

Waller (1992) provides another explanation for this phenomenon by focusing on the appointment and confirmation process when the same party does not hold control of the Senate and the presidency. He argues that under the circumstances of divided government, the structure of the confirmation process is such that "the incentive to reject nominees becomes stronger as the next election approaches, [and] more moderate nominees are needed to placate the opposition" (424).

Regardless of the relative accuracy of these individual explanations, the empirical evidence warrants one simple conclusion: by the time presidents are in a position to pack the board, political pressures prevent them from appointing reliable governors. These political pressures were particularly problematic for Nixon and Ford; two of Nixon's five appointees were unreliable (as determined by Havrilesky and Gildea 1990 and Havrilesky 1995), and three of Ford's five appointees were unreliable. In fact, if presidents are only credited for reliable appointees, the data presented previously grossly overestimate the president's level of support on the Board of Governors and the FOMC.

Consider the data presented in table 5.4. If presidents are only credited with reliable appointees—professional economists, in this case—then no president has ever filled all the seats on the Board of Governors with his own reliable appointees. In fact, only Carter, Reagan, and Clinton have ever appointed reliable governors to a majority of the seats on the board.

A quick overview of tables 5.5 and 5.6 also demonstrates the limitations faced by presidents in the use of the appointment power. If presidents are only credited for reliable appointees or the reliable appointees of fellow partisans, it takes a very long time to make appointments to a majority of the seats on the Board of Governors. Without the inclusion of appointees of fellow partisans, it takes more than two full terms for presidents to appoint a majority of the Board of Governors. Even when including the

TABLE 5.4. Presidents and Seats Filled on the Board of Governors by Economists, 1953–1996

Eisenhower	1
Kennedy	2
Johnson	3
Nixon	3
Ford	2
Carter	4
Reagan	5
Bush	3
Clinton	4

Note: Individual presidents are given credit for one appointment per seat. Eisenhower, Carter, and Reagan all made double appointments to single seats. When presidents reappoint appointees of previous presidents, the reappointing president gets credit for the governor at the point of reappointment.

TABLE 5.5. Number of Months Each President Had Own Reliable Appointees in 0, 1–3, 4–6, or 7 Seats on the Board of Governors (not including appointees of fellow partisans)

President[a]	0 seats	1–3 seats	4–6 seats	7 seats
Eisenhower (96)	18	78	0	0
Kennedy (21)	7	14	0	0
Johnson (75)	2	52	0	0
Nixon (66)	52	14	0	0
Ford (30)	3	27	0	0
Carter (48)	13	26	9	0
Reagan (96)	13	47	36	0
Bush (48)	15	33	0	0
Clinton (48)	20	22	6	0
Average	15.9	34.8	5	0

[a]The number in parentheses following each president's name is the number of months that president served in office. See Chappell, Havrilesky, and McGregor 1993.

TABLE 5.6.   Number of Months Each President Had Own Reliable or Fellow
Partisan Reliable Appointees in 0, 1–3, 4–6, or 7 Seats on the Board of Governors

President[a]	0 seats	1–3 seats	4–6 seats	7 seats
Eisenhower (96)	18	78	0	0
Kennedy (21)	0	21	0	0
Johnson (75)	0	40	35	0
Nixon (66)	12	54	0	0
Ford (30)	0	5	17	8
Carter (48)	19	20	9	0
Reagan (96)	0	60	36	0
Bush (48)	0	0	48	0
Clinton (48)	30	18	0	0
Average	8.8	32.9	16.1	0.9

[a]The figure in parentheses following each president's name is the number of months that
president served in office. See Chappell, Havrilesky, and McGregor 1993.

appointees of fellow partisans, it usually takes more than 45 months to fill
a majority of the seats on the board with reliable appointees. Opportunities to fill all of the seats on the board with reliable appointees are obviously exceedingly rare.

Appointments, Confirmations, and the Federal Reserve

It is the responsibility of the Senate to confirm all Fed appointments. Any
particular appointee could, theoretically, fail to win confirmation. Nevertheless, the empirical evidence indicates that appointees rarely have
difficulty obtaining Senate confirmation.

Of the 35 Fed nominations made between the beginning of the Eisenhower administration and the end of the Reagan administration, only two
failed to win unanimous confirmation.[4] However, not all appointees were
uncontroversial choices. There was a considerable uproar in the Senate
over the 1984 nomination of Martha Seger. Appointed to the board during
a congressional recess, Seger was not subject to Senate confirmation.[5] A
number of Senate Democrats were upset that Reagan had usurped the prerogative of confirmation and indicated their displeasure by attempting to
pass an amendment that called for the withdrawal of the Seger nomination. The amendment failed on a 53–43 partisan vote.

Though confirmation of Fed appointees appears to be a formality,
the Seger incident suggests that looks may be deceiving. There is no guar-

antee that presidents will always be in agreement with the Senate on appointments; the Bork episode confirms the Senate's latent potential for the obstruction of presidential initiative. Short of rejection, the Senate can also impede or delay nominee confirmation. Fed appointees move from nomination to a seat on the board much faster when the president's party controls the Senate than when the opposing party has control. Historically, the average period of time a nominee must wait for confirmation is 46 days if the president's party controls the Senate and 74 days if the president's party does not control the Senate. Lawrence Lindsey's 316-day confirmation proceeding during a period of divided government highlights the fact that the Senate does not serve as an inconsequential rubber stamp. Finally, the recent experience of Felix Rohatyn, a Clinton nominee whose name was withdrawn due to significant Senate opposition, demonstrates the Senate's preemptive power in the nomination and appointment process. More generally, recent empirical work also suggests that the Senate has an impact on the president's choice of appointee (see Chappell, Havrilesky, and McGregor 1993; Havrilesky 1995).

Nominations, Confirmations, and the Federal Reserve: A Simple Model

Though at first glance we might think that presidents are unconstrained in their choice of appointee, we now know that we cannot conclude that the president dominates the Fed's nomination and confirmation process. As indicated earlier, Hammond and Hill (1993) argue that the relatively consensual nature of the confirmation process does not, in and of itself, prove that the president dominates the appointment process. As proponents of the congressional-dominance hypothesis would argue, the absence of activity or overt conflict does not prove that influence is not exercised or that controversy does not exist.

   Figure 5.1 is a spatial model representing the ideal policy preferences of the Senate (S) and the president (P) and the Fed's status quo policy position (FSQ).[6] The interpretations of the ideal policy positions of the Senate and the president are straightforward (and equivalent to their interpretations in the model presented in earlier chapters). The interpretation of the Fed's status quo policy position, however, requires further explanation.

————S————FSQ————————P   Fig. 5.1

   The two central policy-making bodies of the Fed are the Board of Governors and the FOMC. The Board of Governors is composed of the seven appointed governors of the Federal Reserve Board; the FOMC includes the Board of Governors and the presidents of each of the regional Federal Reserve Banks, only five of whom have voting privileges at any particular time. When governors leave office because of retirement or the completion of their terms, the Board of Governors and the FOMC continue to conduct monetary policy in the absence of successors.[7] So, at any point at which an appointment opportunity is available, there is always some status quo policy that obtains until a replacement fills the vacant position.

For the purposes of this simple model, I assume that the FSQ is actually the ideal policy position of a single policymaker. I also assume that if the president fails to nominate a successor to this policymaker, or if the Senate refuses to confirm this nominee, then the FSQ will be the resulting policy. I abstract from two real-world complexities. In the model, the FSQ represents the ideal policy position of a single person; in actuality, the FSQ stands for the ideal policy position of 12 people (the full voting membership of the FOMC), or fewer if one or more seats on the FOMC is unfilled. Second, evidence presented in earlier chapters has demonstrated that the Fed's ideal policy position is only one of the factors that determine the actual policy position. For the purposes of the appointment model, I assume that the Fed appointee, once chosen, sets policy without constraint.

With regard to the first simplification, the impact of a single new governor on Fed policy-making would be difficult to discern if one modeled the Fed as a multimember policy-making body. I choose, for now, to abstract from the complexities associated with formally characterizing the Fed as a multimember policy-making body. While this simplification could, theoretically, be avoided by constructing a more complex model, it is unclear that the theoretical payoff would warrant the additional complications. As far as the second overt simplification is concerned, the complexity of the monetary policy-making process is such that learning about the nomination and confirmation aspect of the process requires an abstraction from these other real world complications. It is sufficiently difficult to understand the nomination and confirmation process without the added complications that are inherent aspects of the process of monetary policy-making. This said, I turn to the model.

The essential nature of the nomination and confirmation process is sequential. First, an appointment opportunity arises (i.e., a governor retires or a governor's term ends). Second, the president nominates an individual to fill the vacancy. Finally, the Senate either confirms or refuses to confirm the nominated individual. In the world of the model, if the Senate confirms the nominee, then the ideal policy of the appointee becomes Fed policy. If, however, the Senate refuses to confirm the nominee, the

FSQ remains the actual policy. Assuming that some cost accrues to the president when a nominee fails to win confirmation and that the president refuses to bear such a cost, then the only equilibrium strategy for the president is to nominate an individual who will win confirmation.[8] Thus, given the structure of the game in figure 5.1, the individual nominated by the president will have an ideal policy position equivalent to the current FSQ. Obviously, the president wishes to nominate an individual whose ideal policy position is as close to the president's own as possible. However, if the president nominates an individual with an ideal policy position to the right of FSQ, the Senate will reject the nomination, favoring continuance of FSQ to the establishment of the policy favored by the nominee.

Significantly, knowledge of the policy preferences of the president and the Senate alone is insufficient to accurately predict the policy preferences of the new appointee; it is also necessary to know the current FSQ. If the policy preferences of the Senate and the president straddle the FSQ (a circumstance likely to arise during periods of divided government), then FSQ will provide more information about the probable policy preferences of a new appointee than will the exact policy preferences of either the Senate or the president.

Suppose, conversely, that the president and the Senate are on the same side of FSQ. In this scenario, the specific policy preferences of the president and the Senate determine the type of individual who will be nominated and confirmed, as figure 5.2 shows.

————FSQ—S—SSQ————P   Fig. 5.2

In the scenario depicted in figure 5.2, I introduce a new term, the shadow status quo (SSQ). The SSQ and FSQ are always on opposite sides of the Senate's ideal policy position. They are equidistant from the Senate's ideal policy position; therefore, the Senate is indifferent between the policies represented by these points.

In this scenario, the president will choose a nominee with policy preferences equivalent to those indicated by the SSQ position in figure 5.2. The Senate will refuse to confirm any nominee with policy preferences to the right of SSQ, and the president has no incentive to nominate an individual with policy preferences to the left of SSQ, since the Senate will confirm a nominee with policy preferences corresponding to those denoted by SSQ. Figure 5.3 is a mirror image of the scenario depicted in figure 5.2. Again, because of the structure of the preferences of the president, the Senate, and the Fed status quo, the nominee's policy preferences will correspond to the policy preferences denoted by the SSQ.

P————SSQ—S—FSQ———————   Fig. 5.3

Now, if the president's policy preferences fall between those of the Senate and the FSQ, how will it affect the result of the nomination and confirmation process? Consider the scenario depicted in figure 5.4.

—S————P————————FSQ————   Fig. 5.4

Given the policy preferences of the Senate and the president and their relationship to FSQ policy preferences, the president will nominate an individual whose policy preferences exactly correspond to the presidential policy preferences. Since the Senate prefers position P to position FSQ, this nominee will win confirmation. Obviously, the president can use the same appointment strategy on both sides of FSQ. Figure 5.5 is a mirror image of figure 5.4. As in figure 5.4, the policy position of the president's nominee will correspond exactly to the president's own ideal policy position.

————————FSQ————————P————————S—   Fig. 5.5

The implications of these various scenarios of the model are fairly straightforward:

1. If the ideal policy positions of the president and the Senate are both on the same side of the FSQ policy position, successful nominees will also have ideal policy positions that are on the president/Senate side of the FSQ.
2. If the ideal policy positions of the president and the Senate are both on the same side of the FSQ policy position, and the president's policy position is closer than the Senate's to the FSQ position, then the president can successfully nominate an individual who shares his or her policy preferences.
3. If the ideal policy positions of the president and the Senate are on opposite sides of the FSQ policy position, then nominees who win confirmation will have policy preferences that correspond to those of the FSQ.

This model suggests, then, that consequential shifts in Fed preferences are only likely to occur over a long period of unified government. Nontrivial change in Fed policy preferences will only occur when *both* Congress and the president prefer a policy that is significantly different than FSQ. Given the role of the status quo policy preference, periods of divided government are unlikely to see large changes in the character of the Fed's policy preferences. Obviously, the implications of this simple model indicate that the president's capacity to mold the policy preferences of the Fed are constrained by the need to win Senate approval for Fed nominees.

Unfortunately, testing these implications in an empirically rigorous manner is currently impossible. One would need valid and reliable indicators of the president's policy preferences, the preferences of members of Congress, and the preferences of each individual member of the FOMC. Also, the preference indicators must all be measured in the same metric. While recent work by Chappell, Havrilesky, and McGregor (1997) suggests that this type of data might be available in the near future, it is not currently available. Nevertheless, the theory clearly generates important substantive implications that will be testable once the necessary data become available. That the implications are not currently testable does not mitigate the model's empirical content.

Regional Reserve Bank Presidents: The Forgotten Minority on the Federal Open Market Committee

The FOMC, the major policy-making entity at the Federal Reserve, is composed of the seven members of the Board of Governors and five of the twelve regional reserve bank presidents.[9] While the reserve bank presidents do not compose a majority of the FOMC, they do potentially serve as an important minority voting bloc in the committee's decision-making process.

If presidents filled seats on the Board of Governors with great frequency, the reserve bank presidents might have only a limited impact on policy. However, openings on the Board of Governors are rare. In fact, Reagan was the only president to fill all seven seats on the board. During the past 40 years, the appointees of a single president have formed a true majority on the FOMC for only five months—the final months of the Reagan administration. The significance of the reserve bank presidents to the policy-making process might also be quite limited if they tended to have widely divergent views on the shape and course of monetary policy. If the group of reserve bank presidents fails to vote as a bloc, their collective influence on the FOMC is quite limited.

Reserve bank presidents do, however, tend to have consistent and similar policy preferences. Reserve bank presidents tend toward monetary conservatism (Chappell, Havrilesky, and McGregor 1993; Havrilesky 1995; Havrilesky and Gildea 1995; Woolley 1984).[10] In addition, reserve bank presidents are less sensitive to pressure from the president or chairperson than are Fed governors (Krause 1994). With reserve bank presidents tending to form a conservative voting bloc, it would seem that the governors would need to have consistently expansionary preferences to push the Fed's ideal point beyond the most conservative override voter during Republican administrations and the most conservative median voter during Democratic administrations. This realization suggests that much of the variance in the Fed's ideal policy position occurs in that area of the policy space where shifts in Fed preferences have no impact on policy. Clearly, the presence of the reserve bank presidents on the FOMC constrains the president's capacity to mold Fed policy preferences.

However, this concern for the aggregation of the policy preferences of individual governors and reserve bank presidents may be unwarranted if the chairperson dominates Fed policy-making. I now consider that possibility.

A Special Case: Appointment of a Chairperson

A number of scholars have highlighted the unique power of the chairperson in the formation of monetary policy (Alt 1991; Kane 1988; Kettl 1986; Woolley 1984; Chappell, Havrilesky, and McGregor 1993). According to Woolley, "The chairman represents the System to the outside world; . . . he is capable of swaying votes in FOMC and board meetings; he allocates staff resources; he determines the agenda" (1984, 116). Kettl contends, "Since Eccles, the chairmanship has been the unquestioned center of the Fed's power" (1986, 197). Presidents may influence Fed policy-making through the appointment of the chairperson of the Board of Governors, and presidents often have the chance to appoint a chairperson within two years of their inauguration.

Nevertheless, at least three factors limit the influence that a president can wield by appointing the chairperson of the Board of Governors. First, certain political pressures may significantly restrict the president's choice set as far as the chairpersonship is concerned. Presidents must consider the state of the economy, potential market disapproval, and public attitudes toward the current chairperson when choosing the new nominee (Kane 1988). Woolley notes specifically that "the discretion of Presidents in selecting candidates [is] restricted by the need to maintain the confidence of the financial markets" (1984, 116). Kane (1988) argues that political constraints may have prevented Reagan from replacing Paul Volcker in 1983, and it is likely that political constraints were in some way responsible for William McChesney Martin's long tenure as chairman in the 1950s and 1960s.

A second factor limiting the president's influence is the potential unreliability of the chairperson. Kettl identifies specific periods of "confrontation" between the president and the chairperson; he also highlights the capacity of the chairperson to transform the relationship between the president and the Fed, as when "Volcker further established the Fed's independence" (1986, 200–210). Alt (1991) argues that chairpersons have incentives to balance the policy objectives of the current president with the policy objectives of the likely presidential opponent in the next election, since the chairpersons do not know for sure who will be making the appointments (and reappointments) when their terms are over. This balancing act leads to unreliability. Carter's appointment of Volcker is a clear example of the problems associated with the unreliability of the chairperson (see Havrilesky and Gildea 1990; Chappell, Havrilesky, and McGregor 1993). Havrilesky and Gildea describe the problems with Volcker's unreliability as "Carter's nightmare" (1990, 54).

Finally, chairpersons may be in the minority on the board or the FOMC. Other members of the FOMC sometimes overcome even the most powerful chairpersons. Greider describes Volcker's waning influence: "Volcker lost the vote. . . . When the news was announced, it would be obvious he had lost control. . . . Volcker was still chairman and yet he was no longer chairman. . . . Now Volcker was all alone" (1987, 700–701). In an empirical attempt to assess the power of the chairperson, Chappell, Havrilesky, and McGregor (1993) find no evidence of anything resembling dictatorial power over FOMC decision-making. Krause's (1994) work is also consistent with this conclusion. Thus, a chairperson's influence fundamentally depends on the acquiescence and support of colleagues. So, from the president's vantage point, the power to appoint the Fed Chairperson is far from sufficient to control the Fed.

Conclusion

Presidents face at least three important obstacles when they attempt to influence monetary policy-making via the appointment power. Appointment opportunities are infrequent; the Senate may be unamenable to the confirmation of the president's appointee, and appointees are often unreliable. Thus, the use of the appointment power is not likely to be an effective means of influencing the character of monetary policy.

The model presented in this chapter highlights the importance of the relationship among the ideal policy positions of the Senate, the president, and the status quo Fed in the determination of the Fed's future policy preferences. In particular, the model illustrates the importance of the status quo Fed in determining the policy preferences of a new appointee during periods of divided government. The significance of the status quo, the nature of the appointment and confirmation process, and the presence of a significant number of generally conservative reserve bank presidents on the FOMC also suggests that changes in the Fed's ideal point are relatively subtle and that they tend not to have a significant impact on monetary policy.

CHAPTER 6

Theory Meets Data: An Analysis of the Implications of the Multi-Institutional Theory

Much of the book, to this point, is explicitly theoretical. The book's theoretical focus should not, however, obscure the work's inherently empirical dimension. Plainly put, the value of the multi-institutional theory is a function of its ability to explain the real world of monetary policy-making. The nexus between actual monetary policy-making and the model is of primary importance. The case study at the end of chapter 3 briefly illustrates the multi-institutional theory's potential explanatory power, but it is no more than an anecdotal application of the theory to a relatively limited time period. The empirical relevance of the multi-institutional theory over a significant period of time has yet to be rigorously demonstrated. Consequently, a more substantial testing of the theory is warranted and is the focus of this chapter. The tests presented here offer compelling evidence for the empirical validity of the multi-institutional theory sketched out and detailed in previous chapters.

That said, I would like to revisit the multi-institutional model to clearly specify its empirically testable implications. One of the foundations of the multi-institutional model is that the Fed wishes to avoid restriction of its independence through legislative sanction. To avoid sanction, the Fed must be sensitive to the policy preferences of members of Congress and the president. Knowing the optimal policy positions and the override points for both houses of Congress and the optimal policy position of the president, the Fed can then determine the punishment-proof policy position nearest its own ideal point. For example, given the distribution of policy preferences illustrated in figure 6.1, the Fed will choose point HO2 as the actual policy position. If the Fed chooses an actual policy position to the right of HO2, Congress can censure the Fed and establish HO2 as the actual policy position. And since HO2 is a punishment-proof position, the Fed has no incentive to choose a policy further from its own ideal point.

———SO1———HO1—S—H———SO2———HO2———F,P   Fig. 6.1

It should be clear from chapter 3 that the actual policy position chosen by the Fed will change if the more conservative house's ideal policy position changes (and with it the override points), or if the president's ideal position changes. Thus, if the House is the more conservative chamber and its preferences become more expansionary (meaning that H, HO1, and HO2 move to the left), then the Fed's actual policy position will shift to the left. Movement of the president's ideal policy position would also result in a change in the Fed's choice of policy, as figure 6.2 shows. If the president's ideal policy position shifts to the left, then the Fed will choose point H as its new policy position.

P—SO1——HO1—S—H——SO2——HO2——F   Fig. 6.2

In both cases, changes in the preferences of political actors have an instrumental impact on Fed policy choice.

One of the most interesting aspects of the scenarios presented above is that changes in the policy preferences of the more expansionist-minded chamber—in this case the Senate—have no impact on Fed policy-making. As long as the Senate prefers looser monetary policy than does the House (i.e., S is to the left of H, SO1 is to the left of HO1, and SO2 is to the left of HO2), then changes in the Senate's preferences will have no impact on Fed policy activity. In general, the Fed is responsive to the chamber that has policy preferences closest to its own. If the Senate favored more restrictive monetary policy than did the House, the Fed would respond to changes in the policy preferences of the Senate rather than of the House.

For the purposes of the analysis presented in this chapter, I assume that the president's ideal policy position is either (1) at least as conservative as that of the most conservative override voter in either house or (2) at least as liberal as that of the most liberal median voter. This assumption is consistent with the formal representation of presidential policy preferences in chapters 3 and 4 and also enables the empirical representation of the distinctiveness traditionally attributed to Democratic and Republican presidents. As chapter 3 alluded, one of the most prominent empirical findings in the literature on monetary policy-making is the relationship between presidential partisanship and the ease or tightness of monetary policy; monetary policy is significantly tighter during Republican administrations than it is during Democratic administrations (see Alesina and Sachs 1988; Havrilesky 1987; Hibbs 1977, 1987, 1994). Likewise, the coexistence of Republicans and Democrats in both houses weighs against either house taking more extreme views than the president. I assume that Democratic presidents favor easier monetary policies than the most liberal median voter in either chamber and that Republican presidents favor tighter monetary policies than the most conservative override voter in either chamber. Thus, for analytical purposes, the president's policy preferences are solely a function of partisanship.

More specifically, the basic multi-institutional theory generates three implications:

1. The actual policy positions chosen by the Fed will reflect the president's monetary policy preferences. Monetary policy will tighten (loosen) as presidential policy preferences become more restrictive (less restrictive), ceteris paribus.
2. The actual policy positions chosen by the Fed will reflect the monetary policy preferences of the more conservative house. If the president is Republican, shifts in the policy preferences of the most conservative override voter will be reflected in actual policy. During a Democratic administration, shifts in the policy preferences of the more conservative median voter will be reflected in actual policy.
3. The monetary policy preferences of the more expansionist-minded chamber will not be reflected in actual monetary policy.

In the multi-institutional model, there is always what can be referred to as a pivot point: the preference point on which policy changes depend. Given any distribution of congressional and presidential preferences, there is some point that is nearest to the Fed's ideal policy position yet is not so conservative as to incite sanctions if the Fed chooses it as the actual policy position. This point is either the policy position of the most conservative override voter or the most conservative median voter, depending on the policy preferences (partisanship) of the president. During Republican administrations, monetary policy should vary with the preferences of the most conservative override voter. During Democratic administrations, monetary policy should vary with the preferences of the most conservative median voter. When Republican presidents replace Democratic presidents, the shift in policy should reflect the jump from the most conservative median voter to the most conservative override voter. When Democratic presidents replace Republican presidents, the shift in policy should reflect the jump from the most conservative override voter to the most conservative median voter.

Strictly speaking, these implications depend on the substance (conservatism) and stability of Fed policy preferences. As chapter 4 illustrated, considerable variance in Fed policy preferences may eliminate the direct relationship between actual monetary policy and shifts in the policy preferences of members of Congress and the president. Although changes in the preferences of elected officials will never be inversely related to shifts in policy, under certain circumstances there may be no relationship between preference shifts and policy changes. Nevertheless, the treatment of the appointment and confirmation process in chapter 5 suggests that Fed policy preferences will remain rather conservative and rather stable. The imposition of nonprohibitive costs on congressional action does not alter the basic relationships identified in these implications.

To test the multi-institutional theory, then, one must have an indicator of shifts in the pivot point. Assuming that Republican presidents tend to be staunchly conservative in their views on monetary policy and that Democratic presidents tend to be staunchly liberal in their views on monetary policy, one can identify the pivot point in any policy-making situation as long as there is an available indicator of the monetary policy preferences of the members of both the House and the Senate. Using annual roll-call voting scores from Americans for Democratic Action (ADA)—a choice justified in the following section—I construct a pivot variable that taps the character of the political environment that the Fed faces when it makes policy choices. The next section describes other variables included in the analysis and the methodology used to conduct the analysis.

Data and Methodology

The methodology used for this analysis—the reaction function—is a common component of much of the econometric literature on monetary policy-making.[1] The rationale for the use of reaction functions to investigate the impact of economic and political factors on monetary policy is straightforward. According to Havrilesky,

> A conventional reaction function estimates how policymakers react to measures of the state of the economy as well as to other variables which reflect political or partisanship considerations. Therefore, reaction functions typically relate a policy instrument or policy control variable, as a dependent variable, to the state of the economy variables that the policymaker is ultimately seeking to affect. (1995, 202–3)

Therefore, if certain economic or political factors have a significant impact on monetary policy, then shifts in these variables should be related to changes in the indicator of monetary policy in the reaction function.

Reaction functions, not surprisingly, have their difficulties. Of the methodological problems associated with the use of reaction functions, two are particularly troublesome in the present context—measurement of the explanatory variables and the robustness of coefficient estimates over time.

The reaction-function literature is based on the assumption that policymakers estimate future values of relevant economic variables to make policy decisions. Though the use of single-lagged values of independent variables as indicators of the predicted values is common (Caporale and Grier 1993; Grier 1991), these predictions are based on an unnecessarily limited information set that is likely to generate inconsistent coefficient estimates (see Abrams, Froyen, and Waud 1980). The use of contemporaneous values of the independent variables as proxies for the predicted values—in essence, perfect predictions—is equally if not more problematic because it generates endogeneity or simultaneity bias in the coefficients (Abrams, Froyen, and Waud 1980). To avoid the problems associated with the use of contemporaneous or single-lagged values of the independent variables, I utilize a polynomial distributed-lag model to generate predicted values for all economic independent variables using multiple past values of the variables themselves.[2] My methodology is very similar to the manner in which Havrilesky (1995) calculates predicted values for the explanatory variables in his analyses. It is important to note, however, that the substantive results presented later in the chapter are not a function or artifact of this particular prediction technique. Comparable results are generated with the simpler—though less methodologically rigorous—single-lag methodology.

The problem of nonrobustness of estimates over time is somewhat more difficult to address. The assumption that the structure of the economy and the nature of economic interrelationships is stable over time is one of the foundations of reaction-function analysis. On an even more fundamental level, the assumption of constant coefficients is one of the foundations of conventional OLS regression analysis. Unfortunately, the longer the time period, the less tenable the assumption. In fact, it is almost certainly true that one can have little or no confidence in the stability of reaction-function coefficients across the entire postaccord period (see Froyen, Havrilesky, and Waud 1997; Khoury 1990). I address this problem in two ways. First, I limit my analysis to the 1972–95 period, approximately half of the postaccord era.[3] Second, I statistically evaluate the stability of the coefficient estimates for this period.

I focus on the 1972–95 period for several reasons. First, as previously stated, the problems associated with the instability of coefficient estimates would increase significantly if I included the entire postaccord period in my analysis. The macroeconomic impact of domestic policy initiatives like the Great Society programs and Nixon's New Economic Policy and international crises such as the Vietnam War was substantial, and the relationships between important macroeconomic variables simply was not stable between 1952 and 1995 (see Froyen, Havrilesky, and Waud 1997; Havrilesky 1995).

Second, I chose 1972 as the starting date because it was the first calendar year after the United States left the gold standard. From a macroeconomic perspective, this was a significant institutional change. While it may be difficult even now to make an explicit empirical connection between exchange rates and monetary policy indicators, the presumption that a structural change of this magnitude would not affect monetary policy-making seems unreasonable. I could just as easily have chosen to begin in 1973 (the first year after the end of price controls) or 1974 (the first year after the oil price shock), but the results do not differ for either of these time periods, so I have decided to start with 1972.

Third, changes in operating procedures at the Fed—a shift from an emphasis on reserve requirements to manipulation of the nominal monetary base—also suggest one could not reasonably assume that the structure of the monetary policy-making environment was stable during the entire postaccord period (see Timberlake 1993). While one might credibly argue that the policy target during my time period—except for the monetary interregnum from 1979–82—was the Fed Funds rate, one would have considerable more difficulty making the argument for earlier time periods.

Finally, the nature of the construction of ADA scores—the indicator of congressional policy preferences—was not constant across the entire postaccord period. ADA began publishing voting scores for members of Congress in 1947. At this time, one of the group's main interests was in civil-rights policy. Not surprisingly, the votes it incorporated in its calculations were often taken on civil rights issues. As time passed, and certainly by the early 1970s, a wider variety of policy issues—including economic issues—became more prominent components of the vote scores. Thus, ADA scores during the 1950s and 1960s might be less accurate indicators of the economic policy preferences of members of Congress than were the ADA scores from the 1970s, 1980s, and 1990s.

In any case, the 1972–95 era spans more than two decades and is a significant time period in its own right. Demonstrating that the multi-institutional theory provides insight into monetary policy-making during this time period is no mean achievement, though it is, admittedly, not the same as illustrating the relevance of the theory for the entire postaccord era. At the very least, the 1972–95 period is a reasonable place to start testing the multi-institutional model.

Even within the 1972–95 period, it is quite possible that the underlying nature of the macroeconomic environment changed in such a way as to generate instability in reaction-function coefficient estimates. The most significant monetary policy-making event during this time was the shift to monetary aggregate targeting beginning in October 1979 and ending in October 1982. To test for a level shift in the dependent variable in the reaction-function estimations, I included a dummy variable for the monetary aggregate targeting period.

Although the use of reaction functions is problematic for a number of reasons, I have addressed the most pressing difficulties. For those interested in the quantitative investigation of monetary policy-making, no viable option to the use of reaction functions—even with all of their problems—exists. I agree with Woolley's contention concerning the study of the politics of monetary policy-making: "There is no alternative for quantitative scholars to estimating reaction functions" (1994, 71). I now move to a description of the analysis and the variables used in it.

In this analysis, I use the average monthly ex post real Fed Funds rate as the dependent variable.[4] The following equation was used to calculate this real Fed Funds rate:

$$REALFF_t = FEDFUNDS_t - DCPI_t \qquad (1)$$

$REALFF_t$ is the ex post real Fed Funds rate for time period t; $FEDFUNDS_t$ is the actual mean Fed Funds rate for period t; and $DCPI_t$ is the annualized inflation rate (change in the consumer price index) for period t. The "true" dependent variable is, of course, the expected real Fed Funds rate. However, the expected real Fed Funds rate is unobservable, so the ex post real Fed Funds rate serves as an observable proxy. Arguably, there is a very precise relationship between the expected real Fed Funds rate and the ex post real Fed Funds rate.

According to the Fisher hypothesis, one should expect to find the following relationship among nominal interest rates (I_t), real interest rates (rr_t), and inflation expectations (π_t^e):

$$I_t = rr_t + \pi_t^e$$

Thus, nominal interest rates should adjust in a one-to-one manner with perfectly anticipated changes in the inflation rate (see Fama 1975; Fisher 1930; LeRoy 1984; Levi and Makin 1978). If it is also assumed that inflation expectations are formed rationally (i.e., $\pi_t = \pi_t^e + \varepsilon_t$, where the error term, ε_t, is white noise), then we may infer that "[t]he observable ex post real rate is equal to the true dependent variable the expected real rate plus a zero mean, uncorrelated random variable" (Caporale and Grier 1993, 6).

The question, then, is what effect the white noise error in the dependent variable will have on the estimation of a model explaining changes in the real Fed Funds rate. First, it is known that white noise measurement error in the dependent variable will not create biased or inefficient OLS estimates of the coefficients of the independent variables in the explanatory model (see Kmenta 1986). However, the standard errors of the coefficients may be inflated due to the bias introduced into the variance-covariance matrix of the coefficient estimates. This may lead to an inappropriate acceptance of the null hypothesis in situations where there is actually a statistically significant relationship between independent variable and dependent variable. As Caporale and Grier explain,

> [W]hen we replace the unobserved expected real rate with the observed ex-post real rate, the resulting coefficient estimates are still unbiased and consistent. If the residuals in the estimated equation are not serially correlated, we can be confident that the only inference problem is that the OLS t-statistics may be too small. That is, our hypothesis tests may be falsely accepting the null hypothesis. (1993, 6)

If anything, the use of the ex post real Fed Funds rate actually biases the analysis toward the finding of no relationship between the relevant political variables and the dependent variable. Thus, finding a significant relationship between these important political variables and the real Fed Funds rate would be doubly impressive. While going through the analytical results, it is necessary to be vigilant for the existence of serial correlation and mindful of the possibility that a relationship that is important may occasionally be dismissed as insignificant.

It is clear that no single economic indicator completely captures the complex character of monetary policy. Even so, the Fed Funds rate—in particular, the real Fed Funds rate—has become the "key operating target for monetary policy" (Krause and Granato 1996; see also Balke and Emery 1994; Bernanke and Blinder 1992; Goodfriend 1991; Quinn and Shapiro 1991). The Fed Funds rate is a commonly accepted indicator of Fed policy, and according to Havrilesky,

> For most of the past forty years the Federal Reserve has typically followed operating procedures geared either directly or indirectly to the behavior of the Federal funds rate. . . . There is ample empirical evidence that over the period from 1964 through 1994, the behavior of the Federal funds rate was influenced by changes in Federal Reserve policy (Bernanke and Blinder 1992). Thus it is not unreasonable to posit that Federal Reserve policy has been the principal determinant of the behavior of the Federal funds rate over the [past three decades]. (1995, 204–5)

Given the prominence of the Fed Funds rate in the monetary policy-making literature, it is not clear what is to be gained by attempting to estimate the impact of political pressures on a significantly wider range of potential indicators of monetary policy. It is almost certainly true that the potential payoff generated by that type of analysis would not warrant the obvious added costs associated with the considerable increase in complexity. More specifically, the use of the real Fed Funds rate as the Fed's target variable is becoming an accepted practice in research on the politics of monetary policy-making (see Caporale and Grier 1993, 1997).

Several variables are used to estimate the extent to which political pressures influence Fed policy-making. First, I construct a PIVOT measure designed to tap the political pressures faced by the Fed if the multi-institutional model accurately characterizes the monetary policy-making environment. Given a distribution of presidential and congressional preferences, the multi-institutional model specifies a point—a median voter point or an override point—that is the optimal policy for the Fed given the sanction-avoidance constraint. This point corresponds to the policy preferences of a particular member or set of members of one chamber of Congress. Using ADA scores as an indicator of the policy preferences of each member of Congress, the pivot point can be associated with a specific numerical score.[5] While the use of ADA scores for this purpose is not unproblematic, these scores are widely used as indicators of congressional policy preferences.[6] Also, ADA scores are the only indicator of congressional policy preferences that has been explicitly connected to monetary policy issues in the extant literature (see Caporale and Grier 1993; Grier 1991). Thus, while ADA scores are not perfect, there is no acceptable alternative.[7]

Table 6.1 shows a listing of the ADA scores of the individuals who held the override and median voter positions in each chamber for the time period of the analysis. For example, the ADA score of the median voter in the House of Representatives in 1977 was 40, several points lower than the median voter in the Senate for the same year (47.5). Likewise, in 1982 the most restrictionist-minded override voter in the House (HLWOVER, the member with the 145th most conservative ADA score) is more conservative (15 vs. 22) than the most restrictionist-minded override voter in the Senate (SLWOVER, the member with the 34th most conservative ADA score).

Taken by itself, this data casts an interesting light on the segment of the literature that focuses on the Senate's impact on monetary policy to the exclusion of concern about the House's impact (see Grier 1991; Havrilesky 1995). In a majority of the years in the sample—14 out of the 20 years in which the median scores were not the same in the Senate and the House—the House was actually more conservative than was the Senate. Thus,

TABLE 6.1. ADA Data Used to Construct PIVOT

	SMEDIAN	SLWOVER	SHIOVER	HMEDIAN	HLWOVER	HHIOVER
1972	35	15	55	25	6	50
1973	55	25	65	40	20	60
1974	52	19	71	30	17	52
1975	55.5	22	72	53	26	75
1976	45	25	60	40	15	60
1977	47.5	25	65	40	15	55
1978	45	25	55	35	20	50
1979	37	21	53	37	16	63
1980	45	25	65	39	22	61
1981	35	15	55	30	15	55
1982	50	22	65	35	15	65
1983	40	20	65	55	20	80
1984	50	25	65	50	20	70
1985	35	10	60	42.5	15	65
1986	40	15	65	45	20	70
1987	60	30	75	56	24	80
1988	55	20	75	57.5	30	80
1989	40	25	65	50	20	75
1990	50	28	72	50	28	72
1991	52.5	20	70	45	25	70
1992	65	25	80	60	30	80
1993	60	35	75	55	20	75
1994	60	30	80	45	20	70
1995	40	5	85	25	5	75

more often than not, the House's preferences determined the PIVOT point. So, not only is the Senate-only perspective recently popularized by Havrilesky (1995) and Grier (1991) theoretically suspect, but these data suggest that it is empirically inaccurate. The values for the PIVOT variable are provided in table 6.2.

I also include dummy variables for each of the presidential administrations between 1972 and 1995 except for the Reagan administration.[8] Although it is a point of contention, some evidence suggests that the character of monetary policy shifts in response to changes in presidential administrations and that this change is not completely captured by the characterization of Republican administrations as monetarily conservative and Democratic administrations as monetarily liberal (see Beck 1983; Havrilesky 1995). I include these dummy variables to control for administration-specific changes in monetary policy not captured by the PIVOT variable.

Dummy variables for each of the Fed chairpersons except Alan Greenspan during the time period are also included in the analysis.[9] While some argue that changes in monetary policy occur with changes in administrations, others argue that monetary policy regimes correspond to changes in the chairpersonship of the Fed (Hakes 1990). While the treatment of the appointment and confirmation process and the multi-institutional theory specified earlier mitigate against this contention, I have included these dummy variables as controls. If valid and reliable indicators of the preferences of the individual members of the FOMC were available for the period of the analysis, one could conceivably create a useful indi-

TABLE 6.2.   Values of PIVOT Variable

Year	PIVOT	Year	PIVOT
1972	6	1984	20
1973	20	1985	10
1974	17	1986	15
1975	22	1987	24
1976	15	1988	20
1977	40	1989	20
1978	35	1990	28
1979	37	1991	20
1980	39	1992	25
1981	15	1993	55
1982	15	1994	45
1983	20	1995	25

cator of aggregate Fed preferences. While research such as that done by Chappell, Havrilesky, and McGregor (1990, 1993, 1995) may eventually make this a reality, the data are currently lacking to construct such a variable.

I also include several economic variables in the reaction-function analyses:

PDCPI   the predicted value of the annualized rate of inflation for time period t

PTCU   the predicted value of the monthly average for total industrial capacity utilization for time period t

PUNEMP   the predicted value of the unemployment rate for time period t

PDPIM   the predicted value of the monthly growth/decline in domestic personal income for time period t

PDIFMARK   the predicted value of the difference between the dollar value of the mark in time period $t - 1$ and the dollar value of the mark in time period t.

These variables are some of the most common components of reaction-function studies of the politics (and economics) of monetary policy-making,[10] and each has a compelling rationale for inclusion in the reaction-function model.[11]

The Fed is required by statute—specifically, the Full Employment Act of 1946—to work toward high employment and stable prices. Thus, unemployment (PUNEMP), and inflation (PDCPI) are macroeconomic variables that are traditionally considered important in the calculations of monetary policymakers. I hypothesize that shifts in expected unemployment are inversely related to the real Fed Funds rates. As contractionary pressures (such as an increase in unemployment) are experienced or sensed, the Fed will take a more expansionary position by cutting the real Fed Funds rate. In contrast, as expected inflation rates—expansionary pressures—increase, I hypothesize that the real Fed Funds rates will increase.

Changes in industrial capacity utilization (PTCU), income growth (PDPIM), and the value of the mark in dollar terms (PDIFMARK) have also been hypothesized to influence Fed policy-making. All of these variables are expected to have a direct impact on the real Fed Funds rate. So, as industrial capacity utilization, income growth, and the value of the mark in dollar terms increases, the real Fed Funds rate will increase to offset these economic pressures.

All economic data (independent and dependent variables) were downloaded from the St. Louis Federal Reserve Bank's on-line database, the Federal Reserve Economic Database (FRED). A complete list of variable definitions is contained in table 6.3. As noted previously, the specific time period for the analysis is January 1972–December 1995. Data for the year 1996 are not included because the 1996 ADA scores were unavailable when the analysis was conducted.

A final methodological consideration is the potential presence of non-stationary variables in the data set. Econometric time-series analysis is predicated on the assumption that the variables in the analysis—particularly the dependent variable—are stationary. When the dependent variable and one or more independent variables are nonstationary (i.e., contain one or more unit roots), then spurious regression results can be generated, suggesting the presence of a statistically significant relationship that does not, in fact, exist (Davidson and MacKinnon 1993).

I use the augmented Dickey-Fuller (ADF) test to determine whether the independent and dependent variables contain unit roots. While the original Dickey-Fuller test is simpler, it is not an appropriate test for unit roots in the presence of autocorrelation, and significant Durbin-Watson statistics for estimates of the basic Dickey-Fuller test for several variables clearly indicate the presence of problematic serial correlation. The ADF test requires estimation of the following equation for each variable:[12]

$$\Delta FFREAL_t = \beta_0 + \beta_1 FFREAL_{t-1} + \beta_2 \Delta FFREAL_{t-1} + u_t$$

After estimating this equation, we can compare the t-statistic for β_1 with the table of critical values calculated by Dickey, Bell, and Miller (1986) to determine whether there is evidence of the existence of one or more unit roots in the variable in question. Since the t-statistic (-3.399) for the ADF test for the dependent variable has an absolute value larger than the .05 level critical value for the appropriate sample size (-2.88), there is no evidence of the presence of a unit root or nonstationarity in the dependent variable. Thus, proper inference does not require differencing of the dependent variable[13] or the search for cointegrating relationships between the dependent and independent variables. Since the dependent variable is stationary, no cointegrating relationships can exist.[14]

As far as the independent variables are concerned, only PUNEMP fails the ADF test.[15] Though the nature of PUNEMP suggests that it is almost certainly not an integrated time series—it is, by definition, bounded at zero and 100 and practically bounded in a much more restricted range, and it does not have an infinite variance—it may be near integrated. Given the problems associated with the analysis of near-integrated series (see

TABLE 6.3. Variable Definitions

REAL	$FEDFUNDS_t - DCPI_t$.
LAGREAL	REAL for time period $t - 1$.
PUNEMP	predicted value of the unemployment rate for time period t.
PDPIM	predicted value of the monthly growth/decline in domestic personal income for time period t.
PDIFMARK	predicted value of the difference between the dollar value of the mark in time period $t - 1$ and the dollar value of the mark in time period t.
PTCU	predicted value of the monthly average for total industrial capacity utilization for time period t.
PDCPI	predicted value for the annualized rate of inflation for time period t.
MONETARY	dummy variable coded 1 for the monetary period from August 1979 to August 1982 and 0 otherwise.
PIVOT	(described in detail in text).
PARTY	dummy variable coded 1 during Democratic administrations and 0 otherwise.
NIXON	dummy variable coded 1 during the Nixon administration and 0 otherwise.
FORD	dummy variable coded 1 during the Ford administration and 0 otherwise.
CARTER	dummy variable coded 1 during the Carter administration and 0 otherwise.
BUSH	dummy variable coded 1 during the Bush administration and 0 otherwise.
CLINTON	dummy variable coded 1 during the Clinton administration and 0 otherwise.
BURNS	dummy variable coded 1 during Burns's tenure as Fed chairman and 0 otherwise.
MILLER	dummy variable coded 1 during Miller's tenure as Fed chairman and 0 otherwise.
VOLCKER	dummy variable coded 1 during Volcker's tenure as Fed chairman and 0 otherwise.
HOUSE	average ADA score for House at time t.
SENATE	average ADA score for Senate at time t.
LEADER	average ADA score for leadership of the Senate Banking Committee at time t.
OUTLIER1	dummy variable coded 1 for July 1973 and 0 otherwise.
OUTLIER2	dummy variable coded 1 for August 1973 and 0 otherwise.

DeBoef and Granato 1997), I include the differenced series (DPUNEMP) in the analysis rather than the original series itself. (For a fuller treatment of the issues associated with nonstationarity, unit roots, and cointegration, see Davidson and MacKinnon 1993; Dickey and Fuller 1979; Fuller 1976; Granger and Newbold 1986.)

Results

One can easily see, from a graphical standpoint, that there is a relationship between the value of the PIVOT variable and the character of monetary policy as indicated by the real Fed Funds rate (see fig. 6.3). As the value of the PIVOT variable increases—ADA scores go up—the real Fed Funds rate decreases, which is exactly what would be expected given the fact that higher ADA scores are associated with liberalism. Even in the simplest regression models, it is clear that there is a relationship between the PIVOT variable and the real Fed Funds rate. The results presented in the following equation show a statistically significant inverse relationship between FFREAL and PIVOT.

$$FFREAL_t = 3.911415** - 0.069663 \; PIVOT_t**$$
$$(1.3694) (0.0278)$$

(Due to the presence of serial correlation in the OLS results, the results presented are from a GLS estimation using the AUTOREG procedure in SAS. The numbers in parentheses are standard errors.) For each one (ADA) point increase in PIVOT, FFREAL decreases by approximately seven basis points, which implies that as the individual(s) representing the PIVOT variable become more liberal (have higher ADA scores), the value of the real Fed Funds rate decreases. Even if a lagged dependent variable is included in the model, the PIVOT variable is still signed in the correct direction and statistically significant. See the following equation. Notice also that the PIVOT coefficient in the second equation is close to the PIVOT coefficient in the equation above. (The numbers in parentheses are the standard errors of the coefficients.)

$$FFREAL_t = 4.957362*** - 0.248000 \; FFREAL_{t-1}*** - 0.084109 \; PIVOT_t***$$
$$(1.6469) (0.0586) (0.0332)$$

Moving to more sophisticated multivariate models has little impact on the substantive or statistical significance of the PIVOT variable. In a regression model that includes not only the PIVOT variable and a lagged dependent variable but also the set of economic variables, the dummy

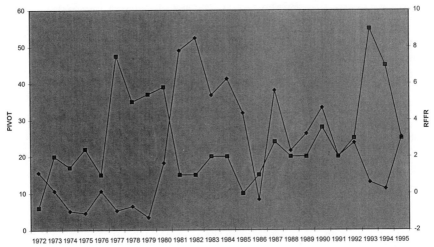

Fig. 6.3.   Real Fed Funds Rate (RFFR) and PIVOT

variable for the monetarist period from 1979 to 1982, and dummy variables for two outlier time points near the oil price shock, we find that the implications of the multi-institutional model still hold: PIVOT is highly significant and signed in the appropriate direction. Again, for each single point increase in PIVOT, FFREAL decreases about six basis points. The results in table 6.4 also suggest that the monetarist period was distinct from the earlier and later time periods, and there is evidence that FFREAL reacts in the expected manner to changes in personal income.

As with the addition of a number of economic variables, the incorporation of dummy variables for each of the presidents (except Reagan) has no impact on the significance—substantive or statistical—of the PIVOT variable (see table 6.5). As PIVOT goes up, there is a corresponding decrease in the real Fed Funds rate. However, the highly significant coefficients for Nixon, Ford, and Carter do suggest that monetary policy during these administrations was somewhat more expansionary than during the Reagan administration. Possibly, this unexplained expansionism is a function of Fed leadership.

Maybe Fed chairpersons dominate Fed policy-making. Although the treatment of this issue in chapter 5 leads one to discount this perspective, it is a viewpoint that is widely held (Beckner 1997; Hakes 1990; Kane 1988). If Fed chairpersons dominate monetary policy-making, then the extra expansionism during the Nixon, Ford, and Carter administrations

TABLE 6.4.   The Impact of Economic and Political Variables on the Real
Federal Funds Rate (1972–1995), Part 1

Variable	Coefficient	Standard Error	t-ratio	Probability
Intercept	4.853125	4.7025	1.032	0.3030
LAGREAL	0.500262	0.0685	7.306	0.0001
DPUNEMP	−0.239306	1.0113	−0.237	0.8131
PDPIM	0.129628	0.0635	2.040	0.0423
PDIFMARK	−0.018588	0.1724	−0.108	0.9142
PTCU	−0.031962	0.0626	−0.510	0.6102
PDCPI	−0.150392	0.1014	−1.484	0.1390
MONETARY	1.990157	0.7177	2.773	0.0059
OUTLIER1	9.306627	2.6556	3.505	0.0005
OUTLIER2	−17.553708	2.7203	−6.453	0.0001
PIVOT	−0.059280	0.0161	−3.684	0.0003

$N = 280$ MSE = 6.752068   AIC = 1344.89
$R^2 = 0.5324$ SBC = 1384.912   DWt = −0.83034

TABLE 6.5.   The Impact of Economic and Political Variables on the Real
Federal Funds Rate (1972–1995), Part 2

Variable	Coefficient	Standard Error	t-ratio	Probability
Intercept	18.982510	5.9029	3.216	0.0015
LAGREAL	0.370605	0.0686	5.401	0.0001
DPUNEMP	−0.078896	0.9382	−0.084	0.9330
PDPIM	0.088482	0.0585	1.512	0.1316
PDIFMARK	0.093839	0.1576	0.595	0.5522
PTCU	−0.201117	0.0773	−2.602	0.0165
PDCPI	0.284113	0.1177	2.413	0.0165
MONETARY	0.522181	0.7049	0.741	0.4595
OUTLIER1	10.492155	2.4497	4.283	0.0001
OUTLIER2	−13.484224	2.5626	−5.262	0.0001
PIVOT	−0.092335	0.0241	−3.831	0.0002
NIXON	−2.720967	0.7417	−3.669	0.0003
FORD	−4.587400	0.6504	−7.053	0.0001
CARTER	−2.372665	0.7239	−3.278	0.0012
BUSH	−0.664910	0.4930	−1.349	0.1785
CLINTON	1.137244	0.8213	1.385	0.1673

$N = 280$ MSE = 5.569168   AIC = 1298.317
$R^2 = 0.6257$ SBC = 1367.445   DWt = 1.28081

may be a function of the expansionary bent of Arthur F. Burns and
G. William Miller, the Fed chairmen during the Nixon, Ford, and early
Carter administrations. One might argue that in comparison to Paul
Volcker and Alan Greenspan, Burns and Miller were relatively liberal.

Table 6.6 shows that none of the dummy variables for the Fed chairpersons affect the real Fed Funds rate. While this finding is inconsistent
with some of the literature on the role of the Fed chairperson in monetary
policy-making, it is consistent with the multi-institutional model. Changes
in Fed policy preferences are only reflected in the actual policy choice if the
PIVOT boundary is crossed. If the Fed prefers a more expansionary policy than the most conservative override voter during a Republican administration or the most conservative median voter during a Democratic
administration, this preference is reflected in actual policy. However, if
changes in Fed policy preferences occur on the conservative side of the
PIVOT boundary, they are not reflected in policy. Apparently, changing

TABLE 6.6.   The Impact of Economic and Political Variables on the Real
Federal Funds Rate (1972–1995), Part 3

Variable	Coefficient	Standard Error	t-ratio	Probability
Intercept	17.695414	7.0600	2.506	0.0128
LAGREAL	0.378306	0.0714	5.295	0.0001
DPUNEMP	0.052347	0.9462	0.055	0.9559
PDPIM	0.095885	0.0594	1.614	0.1077
PDIFMARK	0.092804	0.1580	0.588	0.5573
PTCU	−0.188075	0.0888	−2.117	0.0352
PDCPI	0.310492	0.1249	2.485	0.0136
MONETARY	0.235641	0.7816	0.301	0.7633
OUTLIER1	10.450141	2.4515	4.263	0.0001
OUTLIER2	−13.504795	2.5646	−5.266	0.0001
PIVOT	−0.095212	0.0247	−3.858	0.0001
NIXON	−3.332096	1.2519	−2.662	0.0083
FORD	−5.028759	1.1805	−4.260	0.0001
CARTER	−2.204279	0.9730	−2.266	0.0243
BUSH	−0.556646	0.6697	−0.831	0.4066
CLINTON	1.308910	0.8693	1.506	0.1334
BURNS	0.535761	1.1652	0.460	0.6460
MILLER	−0.876286	1.1271	−0.777	0.4376
VOLCKER	0.189555	0.7523	0.252	0.8013

$N = 280$ MSE = 5.503876   AIC = 1317.732
$R^2 = 0.6236$ SBC = 1387.196   DWt = 1.280814

Fed chairpersons does not generate a sufficiently large expansionary shift to affect policy. This finding is consistent with the conclusions reached in the previous chapter: given the Fed's structure, radical shifts in the aggregate policy preferences of the FOMC should be quite uncommon. Rarely will a change in chairperson alone be sufficient to make the kind of difference that would manifest itself in actual policy decisions.

So, even with the inclusion of the Fed chairperson variables, the PIVOT variable remains highly significant, and there are still significant coefficients for the Nixon, Ford, and Carter dummy variables. Thus, the extraexpansionism of the early part of the period may be a function of a variety of different unspecified factors. This extraexpansionism does not, however, play a role in the substantive or statistical significance of the PIVOT variable. Even if the 1972–74 period is excluded from the analysis, the PIVOT results are unchanged.

As one can see in table 6.6, the PIVOT variable—the variable used to test the implications of the multi-institutional theory—is significant at the .001 level and signed correctly, as it is in each model. Also, the PIVOT coefficient is very stable across the various model estimations, ranging between .05 and .10. This phenomenon suggests that each single-point change in the PIVOT score generates somewhere between a five and ten basis-point shift in the real Fed Funds rate. Thus, a 25-point shift in PIVOT might easily result in a two-point shift in the real Fed Funds rate. These results strongly suggest that the character of the political environment—as specified by the multi-institutional theory—has an impact on Fed policy-making.

On the economic side, it is clear that the current real Fed Funds rate is tied to the previous rate. There is also evidence that economic factors influence the value of the dependent variable. Table 6.4 shows evidence of a positive and direct relationship between income levels (PDPIM) and the real Fed Funds rate. Specifically, as income increases, so does the real Fed Funds rate. Likewise, tables 6.5 and 6.6, show statistically significant relationships between the level of capacity utilization and the real rate and inflation and the real rate. In the case of total capacity utilization (PTCU), the higher the level of utilization, the lower the real rate, which makes sense if one thinks in terms of the economic pressures for further capital expenditures generated by high capacity utilization rates. If factories are performing at capacity, then companies may need to build new factories, which becomes easier as real rates slide. Conversely, as the inflation rate (PDCPI) increases, the Fed will likely respond with more restrictive policies—that is, a higher real Fed Funds rate—in an effort to put the monetary brakes on inflation. Finally, there is little or no evidence of a significant difference between the real Fed Funds rate during the "monetary experiment" and the remainder of the time period of the analysis once administration and Fed chairperson changes are controlled for.[16]

It has been suggested to me that the PIVOT variable is actually tapping into political dynamics that are not explained by the multi-institutional model. The contention is that the PIVOT variable is correlated with variables that tap into the real explanation for shifts in monetary policy and that the statistical significance of the PIVOT variable is simply an artifact of these other relationships. To answer this criticism, I test the impact of the PIVOT variable on monetary policy-making in models that include other variables that may provide alternative explanations for shifts in the real Fed Funds rate.

In the model presented in table 6.7, I have included a CYCLE variable to assess the impact of what is known as a political monetary cycle. Some research suggests that the Fed reacts to the electoral cycle in a way that generates expansionary policies immediately preceding elections and

TABLE 6.7.   The Impact of Economic and Political Variables on the Real Federal Funds Rate (1972–1995), Part 4

Variable	Coefficient	Standard Error	t-ratio	Probability
Intercept	18.257912	7.1307	2.560	0.0110
LAGREAL	0.385634	0.0726	5.314	0.0001
DPUNEMP	0.084644	0.9489	0.089	0.9290
PDPIM	0.096767	0.0595	1.626	0.1051
PDIFMARK	0.080045	0.1596	0.502	0.6164
PTCU	−0.198402	0.0906	−2.190	0.0294
PDCPI	0.330390	0.1294	2.553	0.0113
MONETARY	0.175848	0.7889	0.223	0.8238
OUTLIER1	10.472339	2.4548	4.266	0.0001
OUTLIER2	−13.487963	2.5679	−5.253	0.0001
PIVOT	−0.094532	0.0247	−3.822	0.0002
NIXON	−3.533202	1.2976	−2.723	0.0069
FORD	−5.322063	1.2793	−4.160	0.0001
CARTER	−2.365149	1.0105	−2.341	0.0200
BUSH	−0.469444	0.6861	−0.684	0.4945
CLINTON	1.486795	0.9196	1.617	0.1071
BURNS	0.831836	1.2669	0.657	0.5120
MILLER	−0.608456	1.2137	−0.501	0.6166
VOLCKER	0.273512	0.7661	0.357	0.7214
CYCLE	0.241769	0.4034	0.599	0.5495

$N = 280$ MSE = 5.582823   AIC = 1299.936
$R^2 = 0.6262$ SBC = 1372.697   DWt = 1.085349

more contractionary policies at other times. The idea is that the expansionary policy will aid in the reelection of the incumbent president. One famous case study and a limited amount of quantitative research supports this contention (Grier 1987, 1989; Rose 1974; Tufte 1978).

As table 6.7 shows, the incorporation of the CYCLE variable has no impact on the substantive or statistical significance of the PIVOT variable. The CYCLE variable, on the other hand, is far from reaching any conventional level of statistical significance.

Tables 6.8, 6.9, and 6.10 show the results of tests for the individual impact of the median ideology of each of the chambers of Congress—as indicated by ADA scores—and the partisanship of the president on monetary policy. Table 6.8 demonstrates that HOUSE is insignificant, and, for the first time, PIVOT has failed to reach significance, although it is signed correctly and is significant at the .10 level. The failure of PIVOT to reach a higher level of significance can almost certainly be attributed to the multi-

TABLE 6.8.   The Impact of Economic and Political Variables on the Real Federal Funds Rate (1972–1995), Part 5

Variable	Coefficient	Standard Error	t-ratio	Probability
Intercept	20.445919	7.5667	2.702	0.0073
LAGREAL	0.368465	0.0721	5.110	0.0001
DPUNEMP	0.023911	0.9466	0.025	0.9799
PDPIM	0.106065	0.0603	1.760	0.0795
PDIFMARK	0.107013	0.1586	0.675	0.5004
PTCU	−0.202323	0.0899	−2.249	0.0253
PDCPI	0.284224	0.1276	2.227	0.0260
MONETARY	−0.159135	0.8738	−0.182	0.8556
OUTLIER1	10.637205	2.4584	4.327	0.0001
OUTLIER2	−13.272929	2.5748	−5.155	0.0001
PIVOT	−0.065061	0.0387	−1.680	0.0942
NIXON	−3.205103	1.2582	−2.547	0.0114
FORD	−4.774971	1.2069	−3.956	0.0001
CARTER	−2.660817	1.0728	−2.480	0.0138
BUSH	−0.880412	0.7425	−1.186	0.2368
CLINTON	0.069942	1.5034	0.047	0.9629
BURNS	−0.210955	1.3799	−0.153	0.8786
MILLER	−1.552933	1.3111	−1.184	0.2373
VOLCKER	−0.089586	0.8014	−0.112	0.9111
HOUSE	−0.037337	0.0370	−1.010	0.3134

$N = 280$ MSE = 5.568738   AIC = 1299.022
$R^2 = 0.6272$ SBC = 1371.987   DWt = 1.637133

collinearity between itself and the HOUSE variable. The R^2 of the regression of all of the independent variables—including HOUSE—on PIVOT is approximately .86. Given that this is considerably more than the R^2 for the original regression, there is strong evidence of multicollinearity—a problem that generates artificially low standard errors and the inappropriate acceptance of the null hypothesis. In any event, the HOUSE variable did not outperform the PIVOT variable, so there is no evidence to suggest that the PIVOT variable and thus the multi-institutional model are surrogates for the actual relationship between monetary policy and its political environment.

As tables 6.9 and 6.10 show, in the equation with SENATE and PIVOT, as in the equation with PARTY and PIVOT, the PIVOT variable—and thus the multi-institutional model—outperform the other political explanations for shifts in the conduct of monetary policy. PIVOT is

TABLE 6.9.   The Impact of Economic and Political Variables on the Real Federal Funds Rate (1972–1995), Part 6

Variable	Coefficient	Standard Error	t-ratio	Probability
Intercept	19.734690	7.2971	2.704	0.0073
LAGREAL	0.363349	0.0727	4.998	0.0001
DPUNEMP	0.145576	0.9497	0.153	0.8783
PDPIM	0.101616	0.0596	1.705	0.0895
PDIFMARK	0.097475	0.1579	0.617	0.5377
PTCU	−0.197711	0.0892	−2.216	0.0276
PDCPI	0.291910	0.1260	2.316	0.0213
MONETARY	0.322218	0.7852	0.410	0.6819
OUTLIER1	10.560289	2.4526	4.306	0.0001
OUTLIER2	−13.299440	2.5704	−5.174	0.0001
PIVOT	−0.070997	0.0331	−2.146	0.0328
NIXON	−3.161886	1.2610	−2.507	0.0128
FORD	−5.025458	1.1801	−4.259	0.0001
CARTER	−2.731431	1.0844	−2.519	0.0124
BUSH	−0.767023	0.6963	−1.102	0.2717
CLINTON	0.644655	1.0585	0.609	0.5430
BURNS	0.344715	1.1776	0.293	0.7700
MILLER	−1.086097	1.1427	−0.950	0.3428
VOLCKER	−0.103874	0.7980	−0.130	0.8965
SENATE	−0.029655	0.0270	−1.099	0.2728

$N = 280$ MSE = 5.564754   AIC = 1299.019
$R^2 = 0.6275$ SBC = 1371.786   DWt = 1.622027

signed correctly and statistically significant in both equations, while neither SENATE nor PARTY is significant.

The importance of the insignificance of the partisanship of the president cannot be overemphasized. Although PIVOT and the presidential partisanship variable are highly correlated, this result is not a necessary function of the construction of the PIVOT variable. If congressional policy preferences were consistently conservative (i.e., oriented toward monetary tightness), then the policy preferences of the president would be all but irrelevant. The correlation between PIVOT and PARTY in this sample is at least partially the result of a wide divergence in preferences among members of Congress. In essence, the president's power depends on disagreement among the members of Congress (see Morris and Munger 1998 for an extended treatment of this theme).

That said, these results clearly indicate that the multi-institutional dynamic dominates the impact of presidential partisanship on monetary

TABLE 6.10.　The Impact of Economic and Political Variables on the Real Federal Funds Rate (1972–1995), Part 7

Variable	Coefficient	Standard Error	t-ratio	Probability
Intercept	8.030338	5.6246	1.428	0.1545
LAGREAL	0.406522	0.0723	5.625	0.0001
DPUNEMP	0.015836	0.9672	0.016	0.9869
PDPIM	0.116041	0.0613	1.894	0.0593
PDIFMARK	0.070219	0.1630	0.431	0.6669
PTCU	−0.064656	0.0718	−0.900	0.3690
PDCPI	0.090613	0.1171	0.770	0.4420
MONETARY	−0.000135	0.7819	−0.000	0.9999
OUTLIER1	10.591792	2.5190	4.205	0.0001
OUTLIER2	−14.444498	2.6250	−5.503	0.0001
PIVOT	−0.091622	0.0253	−3.616	0.0004
NIXON				
FORD				
CARTER				
BUSH				
CLINTON				
BURNS	−2.614106	0.5259	−4.971	0.0001
MILLER	−2.927570	0.8516	−3.438	0.0007
VOLCKER	0.446266	0.5292	0.843	0.3999
PARTY	0.663686	0.6446	1.030	0.3042

$N = 280$	MSE = 5.961012	AIC = 1313.681
$R^2 = 0.5933$	SBC = 1368.256	DWt = 0.991683

policy-making, thereby suggesting that the plethora of empirical analyses demonstrating a relationship between presidential partisanship and monetary policy were actually tapping into the multi-institutional dynamic, albeit unconsciously. The difficulties associated with identifying the mechanism(s) through which the president influences policy (see Keech and Morris 1997; Munger and Roberts 1990) are now easily understandable; the theory was always incomplete without a reasonable and accurate treatment of Congress and the interaction among Congress, the president, and the Fed.

Likewise, as table 6.11 shows, in the equation with LEADER (an indicator of committee-level congressional preferences favored by Caporale and Grier [1993, 1997] and Grier [1991, 1996]), PIVOT is significant and signed correctly, while LEADER is insignificant.

TABLE 6.11.   The Impact of Economic and Political Variables on the Real Federal Funds Rate (1972–1991), Part 8

Variable	Coefficient	Standard Error	t-ratio	Probability
Intercept	18.488034	7.8278	2.362	0.0191
LAGREAL	0.347148	0.0878	3.952	0.0001
DPUNEMP	0.312865	1.0864	0.288	0.7736
PDPIM	0.183290	0.0776	2.362	0.0191
PDIFMARK	0.029294	0.1944	0.151	0.8804
PTCU	−0.178644	0.1001	−1.784	0.0758
PDCPI	0.195502	0.1519	1.287	0.1995
MONETARY	0.381066	0.8744	0.436	0.6634
OUTLIER1	10.204471	2.6179	3.898	0.0001
OUTLIER2	−13.693203	2.7530	−4.970	0.0001
PIVOT	−0.108331	0.0479	−2.260	0.0248
NIXON	−2.624301	1.4111	−1.860	0.0643
FORD	−3.881270	1.4869	−2.610	0.0097
CARTER	−0.908148	1.3142	−0.691	0.4903
BUSH	−0.280588	0.7512	−0.374	0.7091
CLINTON				
BURNS	−0.887449	1.5963	−0.556	0.5788
MILLER	−2.180054	1.4687	−1.484	0.1392
VOLCKER	−0.888619	1.0868	−0.818	0.4145
LEADER	−0.014473	0.0131	−1.104	0.2710

$N = 232$ MSE = 6.283606   AIC = 1107.647
$R^2 = 0.6383$ SBC = 1173.216   DWt = 1.957714

For my purposes, the most important finding in the second set of estimates is that the PIVOT variable is still significant, both statistically and substantively. The coefficient of the PIVOT variable indicates that for each single-point increase in the ADA score of the PIVOT voter, the real Fed Funds rate decreases by approximately .7 basis points, and the average yearly shift in the real Fed Funds rate that is attributable to the PIVOT variable is slightly more than 15 basis points. Given the fact that much of the variance in the real Fed Funds rate is attributable to its previous value (another variable in the analysis), the change in the real Fed Funds rate due to a shift in PIVOT is substantial. These effects are, of course, over and above the impact of the various other control variables. Also, there is no evidence to suggest that the PIVOT variable is tapping into a political dynamic other than the one depicted in the multi-institutional model.

Conclusions

No single analysis of monetary policy-making could, under any circumstances, reasonably purport to be the final word. So while the results presented in this chapter may not be definitive, they are, nevertheless, highly suggestive. They provide clear and robust support for a theory based on an original perspective toward monetary policy-making. To understand the politics of monetary policy-making, it is undoubtedly necessary to admit that the Fed exists in a complex political environment that is a function of the interaction among the Fed, the president, and various members of Congress. Other, more simplistic conceptualizations of the arena of monetary policy-making are simply inconsistent with the empirical record.

CHAPTER 7

Is the Federal Reserve Independent?
Thoughts on the Relationship between
Central Bank Independence and Price Stability

Currently, the analysis of CBI and its relationship to a variety of macro-economic variables is of considerable interest to students of monetary policy. One of the central theoretical treatments of monetary policy—the CBI perspective—deals predominantly with the macroeconomic implications of the presence or absence of CBI. This large—and increasingly prominent—body of literature suggests that an inverse relationship exists between the level of CBI and the rate and variability of inflation (for recent statements to this effect, see Cukierman 1992; Alesina and Summers 1993).[1] According to Cukierman, "There is a widespread feeling among economists and other observers of monetary policy that the degree of independence of a nation's central bank (CB) is an important determinant of policy actions and therefore of inflation" (1992, 349). Political pressures apparently force banks that do not enjoy a sufficient degree of independence to choose policies that generate unnecessary inflation. Not surprisingly, since inflation is generally portrayed as generating deadweight costs, CBI tends to be preferred to political control of the central bank in these macroeconomic circles.

The scope of the Fed's independence is a point of considerable controversy. As noted in chapter 2, most cross-national analyses of CBI tend to identify the Fed as one of the international community's most independent central banks (see Cukierman 1992; Cukierman, Webb, and Neyapti 1991; Alesina and Summers 1993). However, analyses that focus on the Fed—and are not, by nature, comparative—tend to highlight the considerable extent to which it is constrained or manipulated by elected political officials (see Alesina and Sachs 1988; Havrilesky 1987, 1988, 1995; Hibbs 1987; Grier 1991). From a purely logical standpoint, these two findings are not contradictory;[2] they are, however, seemingly incongruous.

While the issue of agency independence has been of particular concern recently, it is not limited to the field of monetary politics; the extent to which other federal bureaucracies are independent of the pressures of elected political officials is also a topic of considerable controversy. In the bureaucratic-politics literature, there is little or no agreement on the extent to which federal agencies are controlled by the president or by Congress. Some argue that agencies are independent. Others contend that Congress or the president dominates policy-making. A recent formal treatment of this issue concludes that everyone might be right (and wrong), at least some of the time (Hammond and Knott 1996).

At one level, the level of absolutes, the concept of independence has a certain pristine character to it. At the limit, a distinct and discernible difference exists between an agency that is independent and one that is not. The problem is that while characterizing complete or perfect independence is easy, characterizing limited independence is difficult.

Having described the multi-institutional model, discussed its implications, and presented substantial evidence in support of its usefulness for understanding the political dimensions of American monetary policy-making, I now move beyond the confines of American monetary policy-making to discuss central banking and bureaucratic policy-making more generally. I have attempted to make a strong case for the utility of the multi-institutional model; from my perspective it is a powerful and useful tool. Although the multi-institutional model was designed to explain concrete empirical phenomena, it may also help us to understand the more conceptual aspects of policy-making. While trying to understand Fed policy-making is a sufficiently difficult endeavor in its own right, the multi-institutional model has more to offer.

In this chapter, I use the multi-institutional model to generate insight into—and draw some conclusions about—the more general nature of monetary policy-making. I will also tie my treatment of Fed independence to the more basic question of bureaucratic independence. Through my efforts to address the question of independence for the Fed—from the perspective of the multi-institutional model—I develop an argument that speaks to two larger issues. First, my discussion of Fed independence—whether it exists and what it means—has important implications for the study of CBI and the relationship between CBI and macroeconomic outcomes. Second, the treatment of Fed independence is a starting place for understanding the independence (or lack thereof), and the significance of that independence (or its lack) of other federal agencies.

I find that independence is a multi-dimensional concept. In some circumstances, more than one dimension is present. In others, only a single dimension manifests itself. In the literature on CBI, the term *independence* is rarely, if ever, used with precision. In the more general literature on bureaucratic politics, the term is used with greater precision and clarity, but the extent to which the term is theoretically or practically meaningful is open to question. Using the multi-institutional model as a heuristic for policy-making, I argue that the nature of the concept—and the nature of policy-making—make it exceptionally difficult to use *independence* as a descriptive term for the character of an agency's relationship to elected officials. I conclude with suggestions for a more fruitful means of conceptually addressing and describing the relationship between agencies and elected political officials, suggestions that focus on the use and analysis of multi-institutional models.

The Multi-Dimensionality of Independence

If one were to characterize an agency that is completely independent of political influence and/or control as having perfect independence, what would one actually mean? To answer this question, first consider the nature of the policy-making process, which includes two essential steps: (1) an agency determines its policy preferences and subsequently (2) chooses and enacts a policy based on those preferences. Elected officials can limit agency—or bureaucratic—independence in two fundamental ways. They can influence the agency's policy preferences and/or restrain the agency's freedom of policy choice.

Independence is a concept with multiple facets. The restriction of an agency's freedom of choice is intuitively a restriction of that agency's independence. Seeing the manipulation—or biasing—of the agency's policy preferences as a restriction of independence is somewhat more difficult. It would seem that this phenomenon is something qualitatively different from restricting choice. Yet, in the monetary policy literature, this type of preference manipulation is often viewed as the most serious encroachment on CBI.

An entire literature in the field of monetary policy-making, research on the time-inconsistency problem,[3] is based on the capacity of elected officials—and/or voters, depending on the model—to manipulate the preferences of central bankers. To the extent that central bankers are not independent of this type of pressure or manipulation—because they can be removed from office, their terms are not long enough, or their pay and benefits are tied to their sensitivity to the achievement of goals preferred by elected officials—the pressures tend to generate inflationary monetary policies that produce short-term benefits that are outweighed by significant long-term costs. (See Cukierman 1992 and Waller 1992 for a description of this extensive literature.) I do not intend to go into a long discourse on this area of research but only to point out that this rather less than intuitive component of independence—an absence of bias—plays a significant role in the literature on monetary policy-making in general and Fed policy-making more specifically.

Three dimensions of independence can be identified. The bias dimension registers the extent to which elected officials influence or bias the policy preferences of a central bank. The discretionary dimension refers to the extent of a bank's latitude to choose policy. And the preferential dimension refers to the extent to which a bank can minimize the distance between its own ideal policy and the actual or enacted policy.

If a central bank were to exercise complete independence from political actors in its own policy-making arena, its policy preferences would not be a function of political pressures or influence, and it would have the capacity to choose any feasible policy in the policy space as its actual policy. The ability to so choose implies that the bank would also be able to enact its ideal policy; if this is not so, then there must be some constraint on the bank's policy choice. And if a bank were perfectly independent, elected officials would not influence its choice of ideal policy. So, if a bank were—theoretically—to enjoy complete independence from its political principals, the following would be true:

1. Its determination of the ideal feasible policy would not be biased by the policy preferences of elected officials.
2. It would have the freedom to choose and enact any feasible policy.
3. As statement 2 implies, the agency would have the capacity to choose and enact its ideal policy.

Students of monetary policy-making tend to assume, without exception in my reading of the literature, that independence is a continuum concept (i.e., central banks are relatively more or relatively less independent). Therefore, the literature explicitly admits that the independence with which it is concerned is of the limited variety. Nevertheless, this characterization of complete independence provides a benchmark against which to compare limited independence, a more empirically relevant concept. Not surprisingly, it is more difficult to describe limited independence than it is to describe complete or perfect independence.

Limited Independence: The Interpretation of Bias

One way that elected officials can influence decision-making at a central bank is through the manipulation of the central banker's policy preferences. With regard to the Fed, Woolley argues, "The power of appointment is an important resource [for the president] insofar as it determines the values and theoretical outlooks of Federal Reserve Board members"

(1984, 115). Variation in the institutional specifics of the appointment process (i.e., who appoints, length of appointee's term, ease of appointee removal) are assumed to have an impact on the extent of CBI (see Cukierman 1992; Fratianni, von Hagen, and Waller 1994; Waller 1992; Waller and Walsh 1994).

In the CBI literature, independent central banks have policy preferences that are consistent with price stability. Central bankers are assumed to hold preferences for price stability as part of their intrinsic character as central bankers. Central bankers such as these have been characterized as benevolent or quasi-benevolent and are assumed to have "personal independence" because they are "not subservient to the government" (Fratianni, Hagen, and Waller 1994, 17; see also Neumann 1991).

Political influence, or biasing, through the appointment process is assumed to generate more inflationary central bank policy preferences. As long as these assumptions are valid, increases in political bias may be directly connected to inflationary policy preferences. However, if these assumptions are not always applicable, the extent of political bias present in the policy preferences of central banks may be unrelated to inflationary outcomes. For a concrete example, the case of the Fed is illustrative.

As stated previously, the central policy-making body at the Fed is the FOMC. The FOMC is composed of the seven members of the Board of Governors and the presidents of each of the twelve regional reserve banks, only five of whom have voting privileges at any particular time. The governors are all appointed by the president with the advice and consent of the Senate. The reserve bank presidents are chosen by the directors of the banks they represent.

There is considerable evidence indicating that the policy preferences of Fed governors reflect the policy preferences of the presidents who appoint them; Republican presidents tend to appoint more conservative governors than do Democratic presidents (Woolley 1984; Chappell, Havrilesky, and McGregor 1990, 1993; Havrilesky and Gildea 1990; Havrilesky 1995).[4] While the analysis and findings presented in chapter 5 indicate that presidents are rarely, if ever, in a position to effectively manipulate Fed policy preferences, presidential—and senatorial—preferences do play some albeit limited role in development of Fed preferences. Thus, the appointment power does provide the president (and the Senate) with some means of influencing Fed policy preferences. This ability clearly suggests that elected officials have an impact on the policy preferences of Fed governors, though the findings presented in chapter 5 suggest that this influence is far more limited than previously realized. These findings do not, however, necessarily imply that this influence is always an inflationary pressure.

If elected officials can use the appointment and confirmation powers to influence the Fed's policy preferences, to what extent should this influence be characterized as injecting a bias into the Fed's preferences? One could say that the extent of the political bias would correspond to the extent to which the Fed's policy preferences diverge from those of a similar type group whose members were chosen in a nonpolitical manner. Suppose the FOMC were composed only of the twelve reserve bank presidents and that each president was afforded voting rights. The difference, then, between the preferences of the actual FOMC and the all-president FOMC might be characterized as the bias due to the political nature of the selection of the governors.[5] The smaller the difference in preferences, the higher the Fed's score on the bias dimension of independence. If one could assume that the policy preferences of the bank presidents were always more conservative than those of the governors, then one might meaningfully say that as political bias increases, the Fed is likely to choose more inflationary policies.

If one cannot assume that the policy preferences of the bank presidents are always more conservative than those of the governors, a situation may arise in which the governors have more conservative preferences than those of the bank presidents.[6] If this were the case, and the preferences of the governors were to shift toward those of the bank presidents (due to resignations and new appointments), then the level of bias would have decreased; but the Fed would be less likely to choose a policy consistent with price stability. The potential contradiction between the bias dimension of independence and the traditional characterization of CBI as relating to the achievement of price stability raises a question about the extent to which the term *independence* can be meaningfully used in the characterization of the relationship between central banks and elected political officials. Unless one can assume the existence of a stable baseline (i.e., the conservatism of bank presidents) with which to compare the preferences of the political appointees, one cannot conceptually connect the independence from political bias with the likelihood of the Fed choosing a policy consistent with price stability. It is possible, then, that an increase in bias independence might result in more inflationary policies. So, central bank independence and the extent to which price stability is achieved may be inversely related—a result that is completely incongruous with the CBI literature.

Having discussed some of the difficulties associated with the relationship between central bank policy preferences and CBI (in the context of Fed policy-making), I will now consider the relationship between policy choices and CBI. Most importantly, I will focus on answering the following question: If the Fed realizes an increase in its discretionary and preferential independence, will it be more likely to choose policies that are consistent with price stability?

Limited Independence and the Potentially Contradictory Natures of the Discretionary and Preferential Dimensions of Independence

One way in which elected political officials may limit an agency's independence is by constraining the agency's range of policy choice. Most of the spatial models of bureaucratic policy-making utilize area of discretion as an indicator of agency independence (see Calvert, McCubbins, and Weingast 1989; Weingast and Marshall 1983; Woolley 1993; Hammond and Knott 1996).[7] For example, in Hammond and Knott's treatment of multi-institutional policy-making, one of the solution concepts that they identify is the $CORE_{HC-SC}$. Avoiding an unnecessarily detailed description of this solution concept, one can simply say that the policy area included in this $CORE_{HC-SC}$ is composed of those points that the agency can choose as actual policy positions. In relating the spatial dimensions of the $CORE_{HC-SC}$, Hammond and Knott write that

> the *size* of the $CORE_{HC-SC}$—how much of the two-dimensional policy space does it enclose?—can be treated as a measure of what we might call the agency's political autonomy; the larger the $CORE_{HC-SC}$, the greater is the agency's political autonomy. (1993, 43)

What Hammond and Knott have described as political autonomy, might just as naturally be described as political independence. Or, more accurately, this political autonomy might be described as one dimension of the concept of independence, the discretionary dimension. The use of the term *discretionary* to characterize an aspect or dimension of independence is consistent with other work on bureaucratic policy-making; when Woolley deals with agency independence, he writes of the "range of regulatory discretion" (1993, 109).

The discretionary dimension of independence is readily applicable to the Fed and its relationship with its political principals. House Concurrent Resolution 133, passed in March 1975, requires the Fed to make a semi-annual report to Congress indicating the Fed's monetary policy objectives and goals for the half year following the report. The Fed has traditionally communicated its objectives in terms of monetary target goals and ranges. For example, the report might indicate the Fed's goal for growth in the monetary aggregate M2 is in the range from 3.5 to 6.5 percent (calculated annually) for the upcoming six months.[8]

The Fed currently sets its own target ranges, but what if Congress instead of the Fed set the target ranges? And what if Congress were willing to enforce the target ranges, sanctioning the Fed if it failed to hit the monetary aggregate targets? Under these circumstances, the size of the target range would determine the extent of the Fed's discretionary independence. If the ranges were 4 percentage points, as opposed to 3, the Fed's discretionary independence would be proportionately greater. If the size of the target ranges were zero (i.e., Congress specifies an exact growth rate), the Fed would have no discretionary independence.

Is it possible to think of the Fed as having any type of independence in a scenario in which its principals require it to enact a specific monetary policy? Yes, it is possible for the Fed to exercise preferential independence in this case. The extent of the Fed's *preferential* independence is reflected in the distance between the Fed's ideal policy position (the preferred policy position) and the policy position enacted. The smaller the distance between ideal or preferred policy and actual policy, the greater the extent of the Fed's preferential independence. Even in circumstances in which the Fed has no discretionary independence, it may still have a considerable degree of preferential independence. In fact, if the Fed is required by Congress and the president to enact a specific policy, and that policy is the Fed's most preferred policy, the Fed has complete preferential independence at the same time that its discretionary independence is nil.

Of course, this situation is an extreme case. Intuitively, one would expect discretionary and preferential independence to be directly related; the greater an agency's range of policy choice, the nearer the agency's choice of policy will be to its ideal policy position. The intuitive result is easy to illustrate, as figures 7.1 and 7.2 show.

```
—SO1——HO1—S—H——SO2——F-HO2———————P          Fig. 7.1
         [———————————————]
         range of agency discretion
                   0
         distance from ideal position
```

```
—SO1——HO1—S—P-H——SO2—F-HO2———              Fig. 7.2
         [——]
         range of agency discretion
            [———————————]
         distance from ideal position
```

Using the multi-institutional model to illustrate this point, consider the impact of the change in presidential preferences. In figure 7.1, the Fed can choose and enact a policy at its ideal point (F) without fear of legislative sanction. However, in figure 7.2, because of the shift in presidential preferences, the closest the Fed can come to its own most preferred policy is a policy at the House's most preferred policy position. Thus, the Fed's preferential independence is greater in the scenario presented in figure 7.1 than in the scenario presented in figure 7.2.

The shift in presidential preferences also trims the size of the area from which the Fed could choose a policy that would not result in sanction. In figure 7.1, the Fed's area of discretion stretches from the Senate's ideal point to the House's second override position. In figure 7.2, the Fed's area of discretion is circumscribed considerably; it must choose a policy that is no more expansionary than the Senate's ideal point and no more restrictive than the House's ideal point. The Fed clearly has greater discretionary independence in the scenario represented in figure 7.1 than in the scenario represented in figure 7.2. Thus, changes in the extent of discretionary and preferential independence can be directly related.

It is also possible, however, for changes in discretionary and preferential independence to be inversely related. Consider the scenarios presented in figures 7.3 and 7.4. It should not be difficult to see that the shift in presidential preferences significantly curtails the extent of the Fed's discretionary independence; conversely, the shift in presidential preferences allows the Fed to choose a more desirable policy (i.e., a policy closer to the Fed's ideal policy position). This, then, illustrates the potentially contradictory nature of the discretionary and preferential dimensions of agency independence.

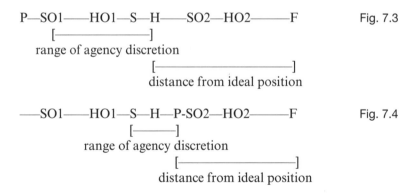

I have one further note on preferential independence. It has been suggested to me that if an agency is required to make a specific policy choice, then that agency is not acting independently and has no independence.

While this is an intuitive and plausible perspective, it is inconsistent with the foundation of much of the literature on the relationship between CBI and price stability. In the clearest statement of the basis of the CBI perspective, Cukierman writes,

> The concept of independence that this chapter [and the CBI literature in general] attempts to measure is not the independence to do anything the CB pleases. It is rather the ability of the bank to stick to the price stability objective even at the cost of other short-term real objectives. This point of view implies that tighter limitations on borrowing by government from the CB make the bank more *independent*. It also implies that, ceteris paribus, a bank whose charter specifies explicitly that the bank's first priority should be price stability is more independent than a bank whose charter mentions price stability along with several other objectives. (1992, 370, emphasis added)

By definition, then, if a central bank is forced to establish a policy perfectly consistent with price stability, it is perfectly independent. In a specific real-world situation, the central bank of New Zealand is required to choose monetary policies that generate inflation rates within a tight target band. The establishment of these bands actually led to a higher independence score on the Cukierman scale (1992). Thus, while preferential independence may seem at some points absurd, it is at these points that this dimension of independence is closest to the letter and spirit of the CBI literature. To the extent that preferential independence is a conceptually vapid concept, the same must be said of the CBI literature.

The Interpretability of Independence: Problems in Search of Solutions

When dealing with the concept of complete or perfect independence, the various dimensions of independence fit neatly together. Elected officials exercise no influence over central bank preferences, so there is no bias. Elected officials do not restrict the central bank's choice of policy, so there is complete discretionary and preferential independence. The bank can choose any policy it wants, even its own most preferred policy.

It is far more difficult to grapple with the concept of limited independence. If independence is limited, than the preferences of the central bank may be in some respect biased by elected political officials. Practically, it is difficult to measure the extent of the bias, and even if it can be measured, it is not clear how to interpret it. Unless one is willing to assume (without empirical justification) that political bias is always of a particular type (i.e., inflationary), how can one determine the general policy impact of the existence of bias?

In situations of limited independence, there is a potentially problematic relationship between discretionary and preferential independence. While the intuitive result—that discretionary and preferential independence are directly related—can obtain under certain circumstances, the nonintuitive, contradictory result is also possible. Discretionary and preferential independence may be inversely related. In a general sense, one can draw no conclusions about the extent of discretionary or preferential independence by knowing the level of the other, thereby making the interpretation of any combination of discretionary and preferential independence immensely difficult.

Apparently, independence is not a particularly easy concept to use appropriately or interpret accurately. Currently, the use of the concept in the monetary policy-making literature belies the term's multidimensional character. At its core, independence is a concept appropriately used to indicate a particular relationship between a bureaucracy (i.e., central bank) and elected officials. While the formal institutional structure of the relationship between a central bank and a set of elected political officials has some bearing on the manner in which they relate, a variety of other important factors (party politics, personal relationships, informal institutions, and so forth) tend to be ignored when the focus on formal institutions becomes obsessive.

The same can be said for the study of government agencies more generally. It is not that institutions are irrelevant. Quite the contrary, they are essentially important. However, to understand why an agency chooses a certain policy or a certain set of policies, it is necessary to understand the combined impact of institutions and the preferences of the relevant actors in the political environment as well as the agency's preferences. One cannot understand policy-making by attempting to understand the isolated impact of preferences or institutions on policy. Thus, the answer to the question of whether the Fed is independent is fourfold: sometimes yes, sometimes no, sometimes both, and it does not matter. To the extent that there is too much fascination with independence, it obscures other important issues, those dealing explicitly with institutions, preferences, and their intersection.

In this chapter, I have argued that there are a variety of problems associated with the use of the term *independence* to characterize relationships between agencies (specifically, central banks) and principals (elected officials). We err in failing to realize the multidimensional nature of the concept and in attempting to write of the relationship between agencies and elected officials in terms of independence as if it were a simple and internally consistent concept. The dimensions of independence are related in complex and often uninterpretable ways. Finally, it is a mistake to ignore the contextual nature of the relationship between central banks and elected officials. The failure to understand the complex, multidimensional nature of independence and the related emphasis on formal institutions have concealed the contextual aspects of multi-institutional relationships.

Undoubtedly, students of monetary politics will continue to use the concept of independence to describe the relationship between central banks and elected officials. To raise the level of conceptual discourse, however, it is necessary at the very least to refrain from talking of a single type of independence; there are clearly multiple types. More attention must be paid to the contextual nature of the relationship between central banks and elected officials. Using the multi-institutional model as a theoretical heuristic, one can see that each of the dimensions of independence—bias, discretionary, and preferential—is clearly context dependent. One cannot determine the position of a central bank on any of these dimensions by an assessment of formal institutions alone; one must also consider the central bank's baseline policy preferences and those of elected officials. More rigorous treatments of policy-making might also include the informal institutions of policy-making (see Keech and Morris 1995) and personal relationships between central bankers and elected officials. Thus, it appears that the relationship between central banks—and bureaucracies more generally—and elected officials is contingent and variable. Misunderstandings of independence have, up until now, obscured that fact.

CHAPTER 8

Conclusion

> From 1776 until now, the money issue has threaded through our political and economic history, and sometimes dominated it. . . . [Q]uestions which are essentially questions of monetary policy have stirred controversy and passions time and time again. (Senator William Proxmire, 1975)

Many believe, as Greider does, that the Fed determines the answers to "the largest questions of the political economy, including who shall prosper and who shall fail" (1987, 12). And for this reason, Americans have argued about the conduct of monetary policy since the eighteenth century. Since 1913, the Federal Reserve has been at the center of the intrinsically political dispute over monetary policy.

In the introduction, I highlighted the fact that the monetary policy-making literature knows no consensus. Some argue that the president controls monetary policy. Others say that Congress, not the president, plays the dominant role in monetary affairs. And some claim that the Fed itself determines the course of monetary policy, essentially free from political manipulation or restraint. There is disagreement not only about the roles various political actors play but also about the relative significance of preferences and institutions in the monetary policy-making arena.

The CBI theory of monetary policy-making focuses wholly on the analysis of formal institutions and their impact on policy-making. The presumption is that as central banks become more independent, central bankers adhere more closely to the price-stability objective. In the case of the postaccord Fed, this theory provides little or no insight into the variance in monetary policy over this time period. Simply put, the Fed has had the same formal institutional structure since the late 1930s; thus, any shifts in the character of monetary policy-making since that time cannot be attributed to changes in formal institutions. Even the accord, viewed by most students of American monetary policy as the single most important event in the Fed's 80-year history, resulted in no change in the formal institutional relationship between the Fed and its political environment (see Keech 1995; Keech and Morris 1995).

When one understands monetary policy-making in this manner, the connection between formal institutional independence and more policy-oriented—and more policy-relevant—conceptualizations of independence (i.e., preferential or discretionary independence) is quite tenuous. The relative tightness of monetary policy has clearly changed over the course of the past 40 years, but for all intents and purposes, the Fed's formal institutional environment has not. In a chapter on the early Fed, Wicker describes this perspective with particular aptness:

> The relationship between the Fed, the Congress, and the President cannot be defined a priori, that is without specific references to the economic and political circumstances existing at the time. The so-called independence of the Fed is always a relative matter. (1993, 238)

The pressure-groups theory of monetary policy-making centers on the preferential character of the Fed's political environment. Shifts in monetary policy are attributed to changes in the partisanship of the president or shifts in the ideological disposition of certain members of Congress. As Havrilesky notes, proponents of the pressure-group perspective "have insisted that monetary policymakers serve a fairly wide array of masters, including politicians in both the executive and legislative branches of government as well as private sector interest groups" (1994, 46). However, the mechanisms through which the preferences of these various actors influence policy go unspecified. Without the identification and description of these mechanisms, it is not possible to determine if or when changes in the preferences of one or more actors will actually result in a policy change.

Unlike the previous theoretical perspectives, the principal-agent framework does attempt to integrate preferences and institutions within the same model. The Fed as agent is assumed to have a principal—either Congress or the president—and the relationship between the Fed and the principal is assumed to be structured by the principal. While this perspective has undoubtedly provided some insight into the nature of Fed policy-making, it is unnecessarily simplistic. How can one reasonably presume that the Fed has only a single principal? And if that principal is the president, how does one assume that the president—and not Congress—is responsible for the formal structure of the institutional relationship with the Fed? What if Congress is also the Fed's principal? How does one characterize a bicameral institution with more than 500 members as a unitary actor? Is it even reasonable to do so?

After considering the extant theories, it is apparent that while each provides some insight into the nature of Fed policy-making, all are unnecessarily limited, and these limitations are sufficiently severe to pose a serious roadblock to the development of more accurate and more useful characterizations of the political dynamics of monetary policy-making. The multi-institutional model introduced, developed, and tested in this book is intended to overcome the limitations of this current body of theory.

Monetary Policy-Making as Interactive System

Hammond and Knott argue that

> control of the bureaucracy is a function of the *interactions* of the president and Congress (and, in a broader perspective, the courts). . . . whatever the extent of constraints on an agency, one cannot single out any one institution as primarily responsible for these constraints. Instead, control of the bureaucracy must be seen as a systematic matter. . . . (1996, 163)

Although I am uncomfortable with the implicit vagueness of Hammond and Knott's characterization of the political dimension of bureaucratic policy-making, their concept of a policy-making "system" is quite apt for the arena of monetary policy-making. Monetary policy is the product of a policy system (or, probably more accurately, a game), the complex interaction of a number of political actors in a specific institutional setting. No single actor dominates this system—not Congress, the president, or the Fed. It is not possible to understand the content and character of monetary policy without understanding the monetary policy objectives of each of these actors and the place or role of each actor in the system. If nothing else, the multi-institutional theory of Fed policy-making demonstrates that an understanding of the political dynamics of monetary policy-making requires knowledge of the preferences of relevant actors within the system and of the institutional structure of their interactions. Both the institutional relationship within which the Fed exists and the preferences of significant actors in that environment must be considered when attempting to theorize about the political dimension of monetary policy.

Neither the idea that institutions matter nor the idea that preferences matter is new to this literature. That the two ideas can coexist—that they must in fact coexist and be treated and analyzed in tandem—is not widely realized or understood. To move beyond the current limited understanding of Fed policy-making, it is necessary to develop and use theories that incorporate both realistic institutional structures and preferential contexts. As I argue in the early parts of the book, the extant literature provides no such theory.

The case for the multi-institutional theory is compelling. In a reasonably realistic setting, it specifies the relationship between the policy preferences of the president and members of Congress and Fed policy-making. It indicates when shifts in the preferences of these actors will and will not influence actual monetary policy, and it stipulates the extent of the impact of these preference changes on policy. It also provides a characterization of the relationship between changes in the Fed's policy preferences and changes in actual policy. And it generates explicit, testable hypotheses for each of these findings. Finally, it holds up to rigorous empirical testing, and through application, it provides insight into the relevance of the concept of independence for the study of monetary policy-making and bureaucratic policy-making more generally. No other theory comes close to generating these returns.

Monetary Policy-Making in a Democratic Polity

If an adequate understanding of monetary policy-making requires a sophisticated treatment of the institutional and preferential dimensions of policy-making and their intersection, what does it imply about the relationship between the Fed and the public? What are the multi-institutional theory's general implications for monetary policy-making in a democratic polity?

1. *The choice of monetary policy depends on the nexus between institutions (constitutional and organizational structure) and preferences (those of the Fed, members of Congress, and the president).*

If one is willing to assume that elected officials accurately represent the people and their preferences, monetary policy is a function of public preferences and public choices. Those who argue that the Fed is perfectly and completely insulated from the public and the people's representatives are simply incorrect. What elected officials want matters—a great deal, in fact.

What is not so obvious, however, is that monetary policy is a function not only of current public preferences (via the current preferences of elected officials) but also of previous public preferences as they are manifested in institutions. For example, constitutional choices made more than 200 years ago influence the character of monetary policy-making. As the multi-institutional model clearly implies, if the supramajority required for the override of a presidential veto were 55 percent instead of two-thirds of both houses, the relationship between the current distribution of public policy preferences and monetary policy would be different. If the president had no veto power, the relationship would again be different.

Institutional choices made decades ago also have an impact on the current relationship between the distribution of public policy preferences and monetary policy. If the responsibilities of the FOMC were actually executed by the Board of Governors (i.e., without bank presidents voting on policy), then policy would likely differ. Likewise, if all of the reserve bank presidents had voting privileges concurrently on the FOMC, then the relationship between public policy preferences and actual policy would probably differ. Clearly the relationship between current policy preferences and actual policy depends on previous public choices. The exposition of the multi-institutional model makes this contention obvious.

> 2. *Actual monetary policy is related to the distribution of the policy preferences of elected officials. To understand this relationship, it is necessary to realize that the dispersion of preferences is just as important—if not more so—than the central tendency of preferences.*

When thinking of the relationship between public preferences—or the preferences of elected officials—and public policy, one tends to focus on the role of the median voter in the determination of actual policy. This is true for the CBI, pressure-group, and principal-agent models of monetary policy-making. In the CBI model, there is no recognized variance in the preferences of elected officials: elected officials are simply assumed to desire monetary expansion. To the extent that a central bank is independent, it can withstand these inflationary pressures. Principal-agent models fundamentally concern the impact of a single principal on the implementation of policy by a single agent. If only a single principal is involved, there can be no variance in policy preferences; there can only be a central tendency. Finally, even the pressure-group theories tend to deal with specific actors or sets of actors as if the only important factor is the central tendency of their policy preferences. While the preferences of Congress may not be the same as those of the president, there is no consideration of the possibility that changes in the distribution of preferences within Congress—even assuming constancy of the central tendency—will affect policy.

The multi-institutional model suggests that the dispersion of preferences—in this case, within Congress—is quite important. In fact, if there were no preferential variance among members of Congress, the multi-institutional theory implies that the Fed would do exactly what every single member of Congress wants it to do. Morris and Munger (1998) have examined this phenomena in greater detail than is possible here, and their findings indicate that the distribution of preferences within Congress—both the interchamber and intrachamber distribution of preferences—determines the extent to which monetary policy reflects changes in the preferences of the median voter in either chamber and to which a shift in presidential preferences will affect the choice of policy. In sum, the distribution of preferences matters, although previous theories have ignored this fact.

The relationship between preferential dispersion among elected officials and bureaucratic outcomes is of special significance from the standpoint of the study of democratic politics. The capacity of federal agencies, including the Fed, to stray from the median policy preferences of elected officials (and, by inference, the public) is a function of the dispersion of preferences in Washington and the rest of the country. To the extent that elected officials (and the public) speak with one voice, bureaucracies do as they are told.

3. *Monetary policy always reflects the policy preferences of a significant portion of the population (or of elected officials). However, monetary policy may not—probably does not—always reflect the policy preferences of a majority of the population.*

Without an explicit treatment of the distribution of public policy preferences, there is a very "all or nothing" sense of the relationship between public preferences and actual policy. For example, in principal-agent treatments of monetary policy-making, either the principal (Congress or the president) or the agent (the Fed) dominates the relationship. This scenario implies that policy is either completely consistent or completely inconsistent with public preferences. There is no sense that a significant portion of the public could be satisfied with policy while another portion would be unsatisfied. While this implication is consistent with the nature and character of the pressure-groups model, the relationship is unclear and incompletely specified.

The multi-institutional model fits neatly into the tradition of democratic theory that Riker (1982) labeled "Madisonian." Rather than clearly and explicitly directing the course of policy—as the Populist traditions might suggest (see Riker 1982)—the structure of the relationship between the Fed and its political environment is one in which the Fed guides policy within the shifting boundaries set by the preferences of elected officials. Thus, those who complain about the "undemocratic" nature of Fed policy-making (see Greider 1987) have a very restrictive view of the nature of "democratic" politics.

Moving Forward

There is never really a last word on any issue of importance. This book is not meant to be the final word on Fed policy-making. More than anything, it is the first word from a new perspective. Given what has been written, I offer the following suggestions as natural extensions of the research and work contained herein.

1. *The multi-institutional model should be extended to incorporate congressional committees.*

One of my objectives was to demonstrate that members of Congress could influence policy-making without reliance on the special relationship between committees and agencies. All of the work in the vein of the congressional-dominance model focuses on the impact of committee influence on bureaucratic policy-making. It should be clear from the foregoing analysis that Congress's impact on monetary policy-making does not require a prominent role or special prerogatives for committees and committee members. This done and said, a theoretical and empirical investigation of the role of various congressional committees (most likely the House and Senate Banking Committees, the Joint Committee on Economic Policy, and the House Rules Committee) in the formation of monetary policy is desirable.

2. *Indicators of monetary policy preferences that are more reliable and have greater validity must be developed.*

This suggestion should really speak for itself. ADA scores are hardly perfect indicators of congressional preferences. Likewise, partisanship is only a rough indicator of the president's preferred policy position. While there have been efforts to overcome the limitations of policy indicators like partisanship—Havrilesky's (1988, 1995) work on signaling comes to mind—scholarship remains some distance from the types of indicators that would allow a specific placement of each member of Congress, the president, and the Fed in a common policy space. For now, it is possible to do no better than to use voting scores (like those from the ADA) and partisanship to make some attempt at placing elected officials in the policy space. In the case of Fed preferences, one has to make some admittedly restrictive assumptions. Obviously, the current data is not completely satisfactory.

3. *The empirical evaluation of the multi-institutional model should be extended to other policy arenas.*

Even though the multi-institutional model works well in the case of the Fed, and even though the foundations of the multi-institutional model are formal models of more conventional bureaucracies, the conclusions drawn about the political dynamics in other policy environments must be guarded. To know about other policy-making arenas, someone must actually do the research. Nevertheless, it is important to remember that the multi-institutional model can be a very useful guide and theoretical foundation for future research in other policy areas.

4. *Scholars should work toward the development of a comprehensive, game-theoretic treatment of public policy-making.*

When we finally construct a substantial and rigorous theory of public policy-making, it will be—like the multi-institutional model—based on game theory. I know of no other conceptual apparatus that will be a sufficiently sturdy and powerful foundation for an intellectual heuristic that must be multi-institutional, multitemporal, and generalizable to a host of diverse policy-making situations and environments. I also know of no other perspective that can adequately deal with the fundamental building blocks of public policy: preferences and institutions.

Bureaucracies and Regulatory Agencies in the Democratic Polity

As I noted at the outset, this book is first and foremost about the political dimension of monetary policy-making. Nevertheless, the case of the Fed does provide some insight into the nature and character of bureaucratic policy-making more generally. First, because the Fed is a particularly unusual bureaucracy or regulatory agency, the effective application of a theory designed for more conventional bureaucracies suggests that the theory is even more likely to provide insight into the political dimension of the inner workings of more traditionally structured bureaucracies. If there is an ideal or exemplary "most difficult" case (see Eckstein 1975) for the multi-institutional theory of bureaucratic policy-making, it is the Fed.

The empirical analysis of the multi-institutional theory of monetary policy-making is one of the few examples of an empirical analysis of bureaucratic policy-making with an explicitly multi-institutional framework.[1] While a great deal of research has focused on the dyadic relationship between federal agencies and important actors in their political environments, I am unaware of any other empirical studies of an explicitly specified policy-making "system" or game. Basing empirical analyses of a policy-making system on a theory of dyadic relationships (i.e., principal-agent theory) and then conducting a multivariate analysis is not—is specifically not—the same thing. (See Hill's [1995] reaction to Wood and Waterman 1994.)

Finally, the analysis presented here suggests a different perspective toward the role or place of bureaucratic policy-making in a democratic polity. To the extent that the political dynamics of bureaucratic policy-making generally resemble the political dynamics of Fed policy-making, it is necessary to investigate and take more seriously the relationship between policy and the distribution of policy preferences rather than focusing solely on the central tendency of policy preferences. While the position of the median voter is still important, the distribution of voters around the median—and, thus, the distribution of legislators around the median legislator—also has considerable significance. To understand the actual role or position of a bureaucracy in a democratic polity—which must be done if we expect to address, from a normative standpoint, the *proper* role of bureaucracy in a democratic polity—we must take these considerations seriously.

Equilibrium Proofs for the Unicameral Multi-Institutional Model of Monetary Policy-Making

In this appendix, I describe the subgame perfect strategies for members of Congress, the president and the Fed. Because of the number of potential alternatives available to the Fed when making policy—and to Congress when legislating a monetary rule—it is quite difficult to provide a concise extensive-form depiction of this game. Nevertheless, through backward induction, one can identify the optimal response function for the active player in each stage of the game. The set of optimal response functions for each individual player is that player's optimal strategy, and the set of optimal strategies is the subgame perfect equilibrium.

In this context, backward induction—also known as dynamic programming (van Damme 1987, 5)—involves working backward from the endpoints of the game and identifying the optimal responses at each stage of the game (or, more technically, at each subgame). Thus, one begins by determining the best response function for the Congress if the president has vetoed the enactment of a monetary rule. Then, given this response, one determines the president's best response function to the enactment of a monetary rule, and so on. Backward induction is the accepted means of identifying subgame perfect equilibria in games of perfect information (see Binmore 1994; Eichberger 1993). For examples of the use of backward induction to identify subgame perfect equilibria in multi-institutional models, see Ferejohn and Shipan (1990) and Spitzer (1990).

The two cases of interest in the unicameral model are as follows:

————O1————C————O2—F,P—   Fig. A1

—P——O1————C————O2—F—   Fig. A2

One can describe these cases more generally with the following:

(1) $O1 < C < O2 < F \leq P$

(2) $P < O1 < C < O2 < F$

The following is a description of the best response function for the active player at each stage in the game. In reverse order, the stages are as follows:

4. Congress decides whether to override veto.
3. President decides whether to veto monetary rule.
2. Congress decides whether to enact monetary rule to preempt Fed policy choice.
1. Fed chooses a policy.

The best response functions determine the subgame perfect equilibria. In reading through the following analyses, it is important to remember that all actors wish to avoid the preemption of their policy actions. Thus, there is a prohibitive cost involved in taking an action (i.e., sanctioning the Fed) that is later overturned (i.e., via a sustainable veto).

Notation

P	=	ideal point of the president
C	=	ideal point of the median legislator in Congress
C_v	=	median voter
O1	=	ideal point of left-side veto voter (the 34th voter in this 100-person Congress)
$O1_v$	=	veto voter at point O1
O2	=	ideal point of right-side veto voter (the 67th voter in this 100-person Congress)
$O2_v$	=	veto voter at point O2
F	=	ideal point of the Fed
f_p	=	Fed's choice of policy
c_p	=	Congress's choice of policy

Case 1: $O1 < C < O2 < F \leq P$

Stage 4 (assumes a veto): If two-thirds of the members of Congress prefer c_p to f_p—or, more succinctly, if both $O1_v$ and $O2_v$ prefer c_p to f_p—Congress will override the presidential veto.

Stage 3 (assumes enactment of a legislative rule): If $c_p > f_p$,* the president favors Congress's choice of policy to that of the Fed and thus withholds the veto. If $f_p > c_p$ and $O2_v$ prefers c_p to f_p, then the president, realizing that the veto would not be sustained, again withholds the veto. Finally, if $f_p > c_p$ and $O2_v$ prefers f_p to c_p, the president vetoes the legislation establishing c_p.

Stage 2: If $f_p < C$, Congress enacts a monetary policy rule c_p that corresponds to policy position C. Both a majority of Congress and the president prefer c_p to f_p under these circumstances. If $C \leq f_p \leq O2$, then Congress does not pass a monetary policy rule. If $f_p > O2$, Congress enacts a monetary policy rule c_p that corresponds to O2, a policy position preferred to f_p by at least two-thirds of the Congress and thus it is veto-proof.

Stage 1: The Fed establishes a monetary policy f_p that corresponds to O2. The Fed prefers $f_p = O2$ to any $f_p < O2$, and any $f_p > O2$ will be overturned by Congress.

Case 2:   P < O1 < C < O2 < F

Stage 4 (assumes a veto): If two-thirds of the members of Congress prefer c_p to f_p—or, more succinctly, if both $O1_v$ and $O2_v$ prefer c_p to f_p—Congress will override the presidential veto.

Stage 3 (assumes enactment of a legislative rule): If $f_p > c_p$, the president favors Congress's choice of policy to that of the Fed and thus withholds the veto. If $f_p < c_p$ and $O1_v$ prefers c_p to f_p, then the president, realizing that the veto would not be sustained, again withholds the veto. Finally, if $f_p < c_p$ and $O1_v$ prefers f_p to c_p, the president vetoes the legislation establishing c_p.

Stage 2: If $f_p > C$, Congress enacts a monetary policy rule c_p that corresponds to policy position C. Both a majority of Congress and the president prefer c_p to f_p under these circumstances. If $O1 \leq f_p \leq C$, then Congress does not pass a monetary policy rule. If $f_p < O1$, Congress enacts a monetary policy rule c_p that corresponds to O1, a policy position preferred to f_p by at least two-thirds of the Congress and thus it is veto-proof.

Stage 1: The Fed establishes a monetary policy f_p that corresponds to C. The Fed prefers $f_p = C$ to any $f_p < C$, and any $f_p > C$ will be overturned by Congress.

---

*By definition $c_p > f_p$ signifies that c_p is a more contractionary (further to the right) policy than f_p.

This proof establishes two of the central unicameral model results presented previously:

1. If the president's ideal policy position corresponds to that of the Fed or is more conservative, actual policy will be determined by the position of the most conservative veto voter in Congress.
2. If the president's ideal policy position is more liberal than that of the most liberal veto voter, actual policy will be determined by the position of the median voter in Congress.*

One can derive the equilibrium results for the bicameral model in a similar manner.

---

*With slight modifications of this analysis, it can be demonstrated that result 2 holds as long as $P \leq C$.

Seats on the Federal Reserve Board

The Federal Reserve Act of 1935 modified the term structure of the governors of the Federal Reserve in two ways. It mandated that the president appoint members of the board to staggered terms that would result in exactly one vacancy every two years. The act also mandated that governors would be appointed for 14-year terms after the initial staggering. The dates listed after the seat numbers indicate when the terms associated with the seats have ended since 1936 and when the present term associated with that seat will end. Most of the information presented here was gathered from the Federal Reserve Bulletin. Seating charts similar to the ones presented here can be found in Knott 1984, although his charts are less detailed and cover a shorter time span.

The date of nomination for each governor follows his or her name. Dates given in parentheses indicate the day the particular governor took the oath of office and the day that governor's service ended. Chairpersons' names appear in boldface. The appointing president is listed, as is the information concerning reappointments and termination. Only those governors serving after the Truman administration are listed. As Woolley notes, "There is general agreement that clear exercise of Federal Reserve independence, came only . . . after [Eisenhower's] election" (1984, 45). Seat 1 was vacant from July 1952 until Balderston became a governor.

Seat 1 (1938, 1952, 1966, 1980, 1994, 2008)

C. Canby Balderston: 8/2/54   (8/12/54–2/28/66)
    Eisenhower (R)   Completed term, 11.6 years of service

Andrew F. Brimmer: 2/28/66   (3/9/66–8/31/74)
    Johnson (D)   Resigned, 8.5 years of service

Philip E. Coldwell: 8/26/74   (10/29/74–2/29/80)
    Ford (R)   Completed term, 5.3 years of service

Lyle E. Gramley: 2/29/80   (5/28/80–9/1/85)
    Carter (D)   Resigned, 5.3 years of service

Wayne D. Angell: 10/10/85   (2/7/86–2/10/94)
    Reagan (R)   Resigned, 8 years of service

Janet L. Yellen: 4/22/94   (8/1/94–2/6/97)
    Clinton (D)   Resigned, 2.5 years of service

Roger W. Ferguson: 7/10/97   (11/5/97–   )
    Clinton (D)   Current member

Seat 2 (1940, 1954, 1968, 1982, 1996, 2010)

Rudolph M. Evans: 2/17/42   (3/14/42–8/13/54)
    Roosevelt (D)   Completed term, 12.4 years of service

Paul E. Miller: 7/26/54   (8/13/54–10/21/54)
    Eisenhower (R)   Died, 3 years of service

Charles N. Shepardson: 2/18/55   (3/17/55–4/30/67)
    Eisenhower (R)   Retired, 12.1 years of service

William W. Sherrill: 4/24/67   (5/1/67–11/15/71)
    Johnson (D)   Reappointed, resigned, 4.5 years of service

John E. Sheehan: 12/23/71   (1/4/72–6/1/75)
    Nixon (R)   Resigned, 3.4 years of service

Philip C. Jackson, Jr.: 5/22/75   (7/14/75–11/17/78)
    Ford (R)   Resigned, 3.4 years of service

Frederick H. Schultz: 4/12/79   (7/27/79–2/11/82)
    Carter (D)   Completed term, 2.5 years of service

Preston Martin: 1/11/82   (3/31/82–4/30/86)
    Reagan (R)   Resigned, 4.1 years of service

H. Robert Heller: 5/12/86   (8/19/86–7/31/89)
    Reagan (R)   Resigned, 2.9 years of service

David W. Mullins, Jr.: 12/8/89   (5/21/90–2/1/94)
    Bush (R)   Resigned, 3.7 years of service

Alan S. Blinder: 4/22/94   (7/1/94–2/1/96)
    Clinton (D)   Completed term, 1.5 years of service

Alice M. Rivlin: 2/22/96   (6/24/96–7/16/99)
    Clinton (D)   Resigned, 3.1 years of service
    Seat currently vacant

Seat 3 (1942, 1956, 1970, 1984, 1998, 2012)

William McC. Martin, Jr.: 3/15/51   (4/2/51–1/31/70)
   Truman (D)   Reappointed, completed term,
      18.8 years of service

Arthur F. Burns: 10/22/69   (2/1/70–3/31/78)
   Nixon (R)   Resigned, 8.2 years of service

Nancy H. Teeters: 8/28/78   (9/18/78–6/27/84)
   Carter (D)   Completed term, 5.8 years of service

Martha R. Seger: 5/31/84   (7/2/84–3/11/91)
   Reagan (R)   Resigned, 6.7 years of service

Susan M. Phillips: 8/27/91   (12/2/91–1/31/98)
   Bush (R)   Completed term, 6.2 years of service
   Seat currently vacant

Seat 4 (1944, 1958, 1972, 1986, 2000)

A. L. Mills: 1/23/52   (2/18/52–2/28/65)
   Truman (D)   Reappointed, resigned, 14 years of service

Sherman J. Maisel: 4/1/65   (4/30/65–5/31/72)
   Johnson (D)   Completed term, 7.1 years of service

Jeffrey M. Bucher: 4/27/72   (6/5/72–1/2/76)
   Nixon (R)   Resigned, 4.6 years of service

J. Charles Partee: 12/5/75   (1/5/76–2/7/86)
   Ford (R)   Completed term, 12.1 years of service

Manuel H. Johnson: 10/10/85   (2/7/86–8/3/90)
   Reagan (R)   Resigned, 4.5 years of service

Lawrence B. Lindsey: 1/14/91   (11/26/91–2/6/97)
   Bush (R)   Resigned, 5.2 years of service

Edward Gramlich: 7/10/97   (11/5/97–   )
   Clinton (D)   Current member

Seat 5 (1946, 1960, 1974, 1988, 2002)

James K. Vardaman, Jr.: 1/24/46   (4/4/46–11/30/58)
   Truman (D)   Resigned, 12.7 years of service

G. H. King, Jr.: 3/5/59   (3/25/59–9/18/63)
    Eisenhower (R)   Reappointed, resigned, 4.5 years of service

J. Dewey Daane: 10/31/63   (11/29/63–3/8/74)
    Kennedy (D)   Completed term, 10.3 years of service

Henry C. Wallich: 1/11/74   (3/8/74–12/15/86)
    Nixon (R)   Resigned, 12.8 years of service

John P. LaWare: 5/23/88   (8/15/88–4/30/95)
    Reagan (R)   Resigned, 6.8 years of service

Laurence Meyer: 2/22/96   (6/20/96–   )
    Clinton (D)   Current member

Seat 6 (1948, 1962, 1976, 1990, 2004)

M. S. Szymcsak: 6/14/33   (6/14/33–5/31/61)
    Roosevelt (D)   Reappointed (2), resigned, 28 years of service

George W. Mitchell: 8/31/61   (8/31/61–2/13/76)
    Kennedy (D)   Reappointed, completed term,
      14.4 years of service

Stephen S. Gardner: 11/15/75   (2/13/76–11/19/78)
    Ford (R)   Died, 2.8 years of service

Emmett J. Rice: 4/12/79   (6/20/79–12/31/86)
    Carter (D)   Resigned, 7.5 years of service

Edward W. Kelly, Jr.: 1/21/87   (5/20/87–   )
    Reagan (R)   Reappointed, Current member

Seat 7 (1950, 1964, 1978, 1992, 2006)

J. L. Robertson: 1/23/52   (2/18/52–4/30/73)
    Truman (D)   Reappointed, resigned, 21.2 years of service

Robert C. Holland: 5/16/73   (6/11/73–5/15/76)
    Nixon (R)   Resigned, 2.9 years of service

David M. Lilly: 11/15/75   (6/1/76–2/24/78)
    Ford (R)   Resigned, 1.7 years of service

G. William Miller: 12/8/77   (3/8/78–8/6/79)
    Carter (D)   Resigned, 1.4 years of service

Paul Volcker: 7/25/79   (8/6/79–8/11/87)
    Carter (D)   Resigned, 8 years of service

Alan Greenspan: 6/2/87   (8/11/87–   )
    Reagan (R)   Reappointed, Current member

Notes

Chapter 1

1. The designation of voting rights for the reserve bank presidents is determined by annual rotation among 11 of the 12 banks. The president of the regional reserve bank in New York has permanent voting privileges.

2. In one chapter of one book on the politics of monetary policy-making, Munger and Roberts (1990) cite more than 60 such articles.

3. See Greider 1987 for a particularly strident argument on this point.

Chapter 2

1. I ignore informational considerations concerning the extent to which the central banks are cognizant of the constraints that they face. The bulk of the relevant literature suggests that the Fed is particularly adept at discerning the parameters within which it may act without censure.

2. Switzerland is also often thought to have a more independent central bank than does the United States. For unspecified reasons, it was not included in this segment of Cukierman's analysis.

3. Cukierman (1992) provides an in-depth discussion of several political "motives" for the undue expansion of the money supply (i.e., the employment, revenue, and mercantilist motives). See the more complete explanation later in this chapter.

4. This line of thinking does, of course, require that the monetary authority has the macroeconomic capacity to achieve the price-stability objective. I will not address this issue except to say that it is one of the fundamental assumptions associated with this theoretical perspective (see de Carvalho 1995–96; Shull 1995–96).

5. The literature on the capacity of a central bank to influence unemployment levels in the long run or the short run is enormous (see, e.g., Fischer 1977; Lucas 1973; Taylor 1980; see also Cukierman 1992 for a summary of the literature). For my purposes, it is only necessary that elected officials accept the contention that some trade-off can be made via the manipulation of monetary policy.

6. There are some aspects of Havrilesky's work that suggest that he was developing a more institutionally sensitive perspective toward monetary policy-making than that commonly found in the pressure-groups camp. For example, his last book (1995) contains a treatment of Fed strategy during periods of congressional threat. He argues that the Fed will seek presidential protection from congressional

threat, which would seem to be the early stage of a multi-institutional model of policy-making. However, Havrilesky's work tends to have a systems-theory point of view rather than a game-theory perspective, which is an important distinction. It is one thing to realize that a variety of institutional actors have a systematic influence on policy; it is another to see the web of interdependent relationships between players in the monetary policy game. In a systems framework, the Fed seeks presidential protection whenever Congress challenges its autonomy. From a game-theoretic perspective, the Fed seeks presidential protection when doing so is preferable to changing policy. If the president has more liberal policy preferences than does Congress—not an uncommon situation—the Fed gains nothing by seeking presidential support, as Havrilesky suggests. In general, Havrilesky's work fits most aptly in the pressure-groups camp.

7. I cannot vouch for the truth of this story. I merely present it as an example of a particular manner of thinking about the political dimension of monetary policy-making.

8. Although Chopin, Cole, and Ellis (1996a, 1996b) question the robustness of Grier's findings, his evidence is difficult to dismiss (see Grier 1996).

Chapter 3

1. Of course, providing an adequate test of a complex theory with a single case is quite difficult (see King, Keohane, and Verba 1994). Nevertheless, the capacity of a theory to provide insight into an unusual case for which it was not explicitly designed is suggestive.

2. Preference orderings for all actors are assumed to be single peaked, and utility decreases as distance from the relevant ideal point increases.

3. Assuming, of course, that the Fed maintains its traditionally conservative preferences.

4. These five occasions also include the support of Fed independence by a special congressional committee in 1921 and the events and circumstances related to the Banking Acts of 1933 and 1935 and the 1951 accord.

5. Eisenhower might have been equally supportive of Fed independence. Given that Eisenhower shared the Fed's traditional aversion to inflation (see Woolley 1984, 45), his support of the Fed's independence, like Ford's, is not surprising.

6. In fact, the aggregate indicator of presidential and congressional monetary policy preferences used in the empirical analyses in chapter 6 reaches its highest level (i.e., most expansionary) for the 1970s and 1980s in 1977.

7. Degen 1987 suggests that Burns was a "major irritant to the Carter administration" because he actively campaigned against the administration's $50 income tax rebate during the first year of Carter's presidency. Burns's continued aversion to inflation helped to widen the schism between himself and Carter.

8. Burns said, "[T]he independence of the Federal Reserve was respected in an absolute sense by President Ford" (*House Hearings* 1977, 128).

9. The data gathered by Havrilesky (1995) indicate that Carter signaled the Fed 29 times during 1977 and 1978; each of those signals was for greater monetary expansion.

10. Whether the Fed's operating policies during this time period were monetarist in orientation is a subject of considerable debate. See Timberlake 1993 for an interesting perspective.

Chapter 4

1. In the depictions of the model, this policy preference corresponds to the policy position at the right boundary of the policy space.

2. The extent to which the president can use the appointment power to achieve monetary policy objectives, has, however, not gone unquestioned (see Keech and Morris 1997).

3. Assume for the purposes of this discussion that the values of individual points in the policy space are monotonically increasing from left to right (i.e., $P >$ HO2).

4. Remember that the president's preferences are still constrained to the extreme points in the policy space.

5. The model is based on the assumption that shifts in House and Senate preferences are in some sense restricted. Specifically, the ordinal distribution of House and Senate preferences is assumed constant—i.e., the Senate is assumed to always favor easier monetary policy than the House.

6. Again, regardless of the president's position, actual policy depends on the Senate's policy preferences.

7. The description and discussion of table 3.1 offer further explanation of the structure and substance of table 4.1.

8. *Prohibitive* refers to extensive costs that severely limit or completely eliminate the probability of congressional action. Technically, prohibitive costs are those costs that are great enough that C would prefer a policy corresponding to any point in the policy space to C plus costs. Thus, when prohibitive costs obtain, the Fed cannot be forced to choose a policy within the override points regardless of the president's policy preferences.

9. It hardly makes sense to talk of the costs of presidential action because the Fed would have no incentive to attempt to increase the costs incurred by the president due to policy activity. Presidential policy activity (i.e., use of the veto) can only aid the Fed in its efforts to achieve its policy goals.

Chapter 5

Portions of this chapter are based on Keech and Morris 1997.

1. See Krause 1994 for a treatment of the group-level influences on FOMC members' policy preferences.

2. This term refers to the unexpected liberalism of Chief Justice Earl Warren's Supreme Court rulings. The liberalism was surprising because Warren was an Eisenhower appointee.

3. It is certainly possible that a president might require fewer appointments to build an FOMC board majority. Given the proper preference distribution, a single vote/appointment might be all that is necessary. This is most likely in situations in

which a president follows a fellow partisan. I discuss that phenomenon in the next section. Overall, Young 1997 suggests that presidents must build majorities themselves.

4. The exceptions are Alan Greenspan (confirmed by a 91–2 vote in 1987) and John P. LaWare (confirmed by a 90–3 vote in 1988).

5. Seger could serve a single-year term under these circumstances. Extended service required eventual Senate confirmation.

6. S is equivalent to the ideal policy preference of the median voter in the Senate.

7. Technically speaking, governors who complete a term are allowed to remain on the board until their replacements are appointed and confirmed. Although most governors retire before the ends of their terms, a status quo policy still exists. In this case, it remains affected by the policy preferences of an individual whose term has officially ended.

8. I am of course assuming complete and perfect knowledge on the part of both the Senate and the president. Thus, both actors know their own policy preferences, the policy preferences of the other, the exact position of FSQ, and the policy preferences of any potential Fed nominee.

9. Technically, all twelve reserve bank presidents are members of the FOMC. However, only five have voting privileges at any given time.

10. It is important to note that the policy preferences of reserve bank presidents do vary (Havrilesky and Gildea 1995). In general, though, reserve bank presidents tend to have consistently more conservative policy preferences than do the appointed governors.

Chapter 6

1. The literature on reaction functions is immense. Significant research in this area includes, among others, Abrams, Froyen, and Waud 1980; Alt and Woolley 1982; Barth, Sickles, and Weist 1982; Beck 1983; Friedlander 1973; Havrilesky 1967; Khoury 1990; McNees 1986; Reuber 1964; J. H. Wood 1967; and Woolley 1988.

2. Each economic independent variable was regressed on lagged values of itself and all other economic independent variables and the squared values of each of these regressors. The models were limited to three lags for each variable. Variation in lag length appeared to have no impact on the substantive or statistical results. The results from these estimations are available from the author.

3. This choice does not mean that the "political" side of the model does not work for the earlier time period. I have not tested the model with the data from the earlier era or attempted to identify the economic variables that would be appropriate for that analysis. The usefulness of the multi-institutional model for understanding this earlier time period is an open question which the current analysis does not directly address.

4. The calculation of the ex post real Fed Funds rate and the justification of its use as the dependent variable parallels the treatment of these issues by Caporale and Grier 1993.

5. I appreciate the suggestion of the use of ADA scores in this manner by an anonymous reviewer of a previous draft of this manuscript.

6. Although some work questions the use of roll-call voting scores as proxies for legislators' ideology or policy preferences (see Snyder 1992; Vandoren 1990), other, more recent work supports this use of roll-call voting scores (see Herrera, Epperlein, and Smith 1995; Krehbiel 1994).

7. See table 6.1 for the ADA scores of the override and median voters for both houses for the time period of the analysis. See table 6.2 for the annual values of the PIVOT variable.

8. Inclusion of a dummy variable for each presidential administration would create a situation of perfect collinearity between the independent variables. Reagan is the excluded category because his term in office was longest. Using other presidential administrations as the excluded category does not significantly alter the substantive results.

9. Using other chairpersons as the excluded category does not substantively affect the results.

10. See, e.g., Alt 1991, Khoury 1990; Havrilesky 1995; Alt and Woolley 1983; Beck 1982; Caporale and Grier 1993; Grier 1991. All of the studies do not include all of these variables.

11. A variable tapping average energy costs was also included in several estimations, but it was never significant and did not influence other results.

12. I use the dependent variable in the example equation.

13. Differencing is far from a panacea even when unit roots exist. For example, differencing prevents the evaluation of long-term relationships among variables. Unnecessary differencing can cause serious problems (see Mills 1990).

14. Technically, no cointegrating relationship can exist between a dependent variable and an independent variable if the dependent variable is nonstationary. However, if two or more independent variables are nonstationary (contain unit roots), a cointegrating relationship between these variables is possible.

15. The ADF statistics for the independent variables are as follows:

Variable	*t-Score*
PUNEMP	-1.791
PDPIM	$-8.630***$
PDCPI	$-3.430**$
PTCU	$-2.688*$
PDIFMARK	$-10.121***$

$(*p < .10, **p > .05, ***p < .01)$

16. Even when interactive terms are incorporated for each of the economic variables (i.e., LAGREAL*MONETARY, PDPIM*MONETARY, DPUNEMP* MONETARY, PDIFMARK*MONETARY, PTCU*MONETARY, AND PDCPI*MONETARY), the substantive and statistical significance of the PIVOT variable remains unaltered.

Chapter 7

1. It is interesting to note that a recent cross-national analysis of the relationship between CBI and the average and variance of a number of real economic variables (i.e., GNP growth, per capita GNP growth, unemployment, and interest rates) finds no significant relationship between independence and any of the other variables (Alesina and Summers 1993). Although CBI and inflation rates appear to covary, the causal relationship between these variables is not universally accepted (see esp. Posen 1993).

2. The Fed's relative rank in terms of independence does not specifically indicate a particular level of independence in an absolute sense.

3. The literature on the time-inconsistency problem in the field of monetary policy-making is just one component of the vast research on the time-inconsistency problem.

4. There is some evidence (Chappell, Havrilesky, and McGregor 1993) that some of Reagan's appointees had maverick policy preferences that were far more expansion oriented than those of conventional Republicans. These appointees are sometimes described as supply-siders.

5. I am aware of the potentially political nature of the selection process for bank presidents. Nevertheless, while it is not a perfect baseline, it is reasonable. If even this selection process cannot be taken as a baseline against which to evaluate bias, then I doubt whether it is possible to evaluate bias.

6. As noted previously, bank presidents tend to have more conservative policy preferences than do either Republican or Democratic governors in general. However, a number of bank presidents have had unusually liberal policy preferences. Using Chappell, Havrilesky, and McGregor's (1990) estimations of the average desired interest rates of governors and bank presidents as an indicator of policy preferences, it is easy to find a number of bank presidents who have significantly more liberal policy preferences than do several Democratic governors.

7. This conceptualization is not, however, universal (see Bawn 1995).

8. The Fed usually provides target ranges for a number of monetary aggregates, including M1, M2, and M3.

Chapter 8

1. Wood and Waterman 1994 conduct an empirical analysis of policy-making in a multi-institutional setting. However, their analysis does not include a specific model of multi-institutional policy-making.

References

Aberbach, Joel D. 1990. *Keeping a Watchful Eye: The Politics of Congressional Oversight.* Washington, DC: Brookings Institution.

Abrams, Richard K., Richard Froyen, and Roger N. Waud. 1980. "Monetary Policy Reaction Functions, Consistent Expectations, and the Burns Era." *Journal of Money, Credit, and Banking* 12:30–42.

Alesina, Alberto. 1988. "Macroeconomics and Politics." In *NBER Macroeconomics Annual,* edited by Stanley Fischer. Cambridge: MIT Press.

Alesina, Alberto, John Londregan, and Howard Rosenthal. 1993. "A Model of the Political Economy of the United States." *American Political Science Review* 87:12–33.

Alesina, Alberto, and Howard Rosenthal. 1989. "Partisan Cycles in Congressional Elections and the Macroeconomy." *American Political Science Review* 83:373–98.

Alesina, Alberto, and Jeffrey Sachs. 1988. "Political Parties and the Business Cycle in the United States." *Journal of Money, Credit, and Banking* 20:63–81.

Alesina, Alberto, and Lawrence H. Summers. 1993. "Central Bank Independence and Macroeconomic Performance: Some Comparative Evidence." *Journal of Money, Credit, and Banking* 25:151–62.

Alt, James E. 1991. "Leaning into the Wind or Ducking Out of the Storm? U.S. Monetary Policy in the 1980s." In *Politics and Economics in the 1980s,* edited by A. Alesina and G. Carliner. Chicago: University of Chicago Press.

Alt, James E., and K. Alex Chrystal. 1983. *Political Economics.* Berkeley: University of California Press.

Alt, James E., and John T. Woolley. 1982. "Reaction Functions, Optimization, and Politics: Modeling the Political Economy of Macroeconomic Policy." *American Journal of Political Science* 26:709–40.

Balke, Nathan S., and Kenneth M. Emery. 1994. "The Federal Funds Rate as an Indicator of Monetary Policy: Evidence from the 1980s." *Economic Review* (1st quarter): 1–16.

Banks, Jeffrey S. 1989. "Agency Budgets, Cost Information, and Auditing." *American Journal of Political Science* 33:670–99.

Banks, Jeffrey S., and Barry R. Weingast. 1992. "The Political Control of Bureaucracies under Asymmetric Information." *American Journal of Political Science* 36:509–24.

Barron, C. W. 1914. *The Federal Reserve Act: A Discussion of the Principles and Operations of the New Banking Act.* Boston: Boston News Bureau.

Barth, Nathan S., Robin Sickles, and Philip Wiest. 1982. "Assessing the Impact of Varying Economic Conditions on Federal Reserve Behavior." *Journal of Macroeconomics* 4:47–70.

Bawn, Kathleen. 1995. "Political Control versus Expertise: Congressional Choices about Administrative Procedures." *American Political Science Review* 89:62–73.

Beck, Nathaniel. 1982. "Presidential Influence on the Federal Reserve in the 1970s." *American Journal of Political Science* 26:415–45.

Beck, Nathaniel. 1983. "Time-Varying Parameter Regression Models." *American Journal of Political Science* 27:557–600.

Beck, Nathaniel. 1987. "Elections and the Fed: Is There a Political Monetary Cycle?" *American Journal of Political Science* 31:194–216.

Beck, Nathaniel. 1990a. "Congress and the Fed: Why the Dog Does not Bark in the Night." In *The Political Economy of American Monetary Policy*, edited by Thomas D. Willett. Cambridge: Cambridge University Press.

Beck, Nathaniel. 1990b. "Political Monetary Cycles." In *The Political Economy of American Monetary Policy*, edited by Thomas D. Willett. Cambridge: Cambridge University Press.

Beck, Nathaniel. 1991. "The Fed and the Political Business Cycle." *Contemporary Policy Issues* 9:25–38.

Beckner, Steven K. 1997. *Back from the Brink: The Greenspan Years.* New York: Wiley.

Bendor, Jonathan. 1988. "Review Article: Formal Models of Bureaucracy." *British Journal of Political Science* 18:353–95.

Bendor, Jonathan, Serge Taylor, and Roland Van Gaalen. 1987. "Politicians, Bureaucrats, and Asymmetric Information." *American Political Science Review* 80:1187–1207.

Bernanke, Ben S., and Alan Blinder. 1992. "The Federal Funds Rate and the Channels of Monetary Transmission." *American Economic Review* 82 (4): 901–21.

Binmore, Ken. 1994. *Game Theory and the Social Contract.* Vol. 1, *Playing Fair.* Cambridge: MIT Press.

Calvert, Randall. 1986. *Models of Imperfect Information in Politics.* New York: Harwood.

Calvert, Randall, Matthew McCubbins, and Barry Weingast. 1989. "A Theory of Political Control and Agency Discretion." *American Journal of Political Science* 33:588–611.

Calvert, Randall, Mark Moran, and Barry Weingast. 1987. "Congressional Influence over Policymaking: The Case of the FTC." In *Congress: Structure and Policy,* edited by Matthew D. McCubbins and Terry Sullivan. Cambridge: Cambridge University Press.

Canterbury, E. Ray. 1967. "A New Look at Federal Open Market Voting." *Western Economic Journal* 6:25–38.

Caporale, Tony, and Kevin B. Grier. 1993. "Political Influence on Monetary Policy: Evidence from Real Interest Rates." Paper presented at the annual meeting of the Southern Economic Association, New Orleans, LA.

Caporale, Tony, and Kevin B. Grier. 1997. "Political Influence on Monetary Policy: Evidence from Real Interest Rates." Paper presented at the annual meeting of the Public Choice Society, San Francisco, CA.

Cary, William L. 1967. *Politics and the Regulatory Agencies.* New York: McGraw-Hill.

Chappell, Henry, Thomas Havrilesky, and Rob McGregor. 1990. "Monetary Policy Reaction Functions for Individual FOMC Members." Manuscript.

Chappell, Henry, Thomas Havrilesky, and Rob McGregor. 1993. "Partisan Monetary Policies: Presidential Impact through the Power of Appointment." *Quarterly Journal of Economics* 108:185–218.

Chappell, Henry, Thomas Havrilesky, and Rob McGregor. 1995. "Policymakers, Institutions, and Central Bank Decisions." *Journal of Economics and Business* 47 (2): 113–36.

Chappell, Henry, Thomas Havrilesky, and Rob McGregor. 1997. "Monetary Policy Reaction Functions for Individual FOMC Members: Evidence from the Memoranda of Discussion." *Review of Economics and Statistics* 79 (3): 454–78.

Chopin, Marc C., C. Steven Cole, and Michael A. Ellis. 1996a. "Congressional Influence on U.S. Monetary Policy: A Reconsideration of the Evidence." *Journal of Monetary Economics* 38:561–70.

Chopin, Marc C., C. Steven Cole, and Michael A. Ellis. 1996b. "Congressional Policy Preferences and U.S. Monetary Policy." *Journal of Monetary Economics* 38:581–85.

Conway, Thomas, and Ernest M. Patterson. 1914. *The Operation of the New Bank Act.* Philadelphia: Lippincott.

Cook, Brian, and B. Dan Wood. 1989. "Principal-Agent Models of Political Control of the Bureaucracy." *American Political Science Review* 83:965–78.

Cukierman, Alex. 1992. *Central Bank Strategy, Credibility, and Independence.* Cambridge: MIT Press.

Cukierman, Alex, and Allan Meltzer. 1986. "A Positive Theory of Discretionary Policy, the Costs of Democratic Government, and the Benefits of a Constitution." *Economic Inquiry* 24:367–88.

Cukierman, Alex, Steven Webb, and Bilin Neyapti. 1991. "The Measurement of Central Bank Independence and Its Effect on Policy Outcomes." Paper presented at the NBER Conference on Political Economics, Cambridge, MA.

Dahl, Robert, and Charles Lindblom. 1953. *Politics, Economics, and Welfare.* New York: Harper.

Davidson, Russell, and James G. MacKinnon. 1993. *Estimation and Inference in Economics.* New York: Oxford University Press.

DeBoef, Suzanna, and Jim Granato. 1997. "Near-Integrated Data and the Analysis of Political Relationships." *American Journal of Political Science* 41:619–40.

De Carvalho, Fernando J. Cardim. 1995–96. "The Independence of Central

Banks: A Critical Assessment of the Arguments." *Journal of Post-Keynesian Economics* 18:159–75.

Degen, Robert A. 1987. *The American Monetary System: A Concise Survey of Its Evolution since 1896.* Lexington, MA: Lexington Books.

Dickey, David, William R. Bell, and Robert V. Miller. 1986. "Unit Roots in Time Series Models: Tests and Implications." *American Statistician* 40:12–26.

Dickey, David, and William A. Fuller. 1979. "Distribution of the Estimators for Autoregressive Time Series with a Unit Root." *Journal of the American Statistical Association* 74:427–31.

Dowding, Keith, and Desmond King, eds. 1995. *Preferences, Institutions, and Rational Choice.* Oxford: Oxford University Press.

Eckstein, Harry. 1975. "Case Study and Theory in Political Science." In *Handbook of Political Science,* Vol. 1, *Political Science: Scope and Theory,* edited by Fred I. Greenstein and Nelson W. Polsby. Reading, MA: Addison-Wesley.

Eichberger, Jurgen. 1993. *Game Theory for Economists.* San Diego: Academic Press.

Eisner, Mark A., and Kenneth J. Meier. 1990. "Presidential Control versus Bureaucratic Power: Explaining the Reagan Revolution in Antitrust." *American Journal of Political Science* 34:269–87.

Eskridge, William N., Jr., and John Ferejohn. 1992. "Making the Deal Stick: Enforcing the Original Constitutional Structure of Lawmaking in the Modern Regulatory State." *Journal of Law, Economics, and Organization* 8:165–89.

Fama, Eugene F. 1975. "Short-Term Interest Rates as Predictors of Inflation." *American Economic Review* 65 (June): 269–82.

Ferejohn, John, and Charles Shipan. 1990. "Congressional Influence on Bureaucracy." *Journal of Law, Economics, and Organization* 6 (spring): 1–20.

Fischer, Stanley. 1977. "Long Term Contracts, Rational Expectations, and the Optimal Money Supply Rule." *Journal of Political Economy* 191–206.

Fisher, Irving. 1930. *The Theory of Interest.* New York: Macmillan.

Fratianni, Michele, Jurgen von Hagen, and Christopher Waller. 1994. *Central Banking as a Political Principal-Agent Problem.* Indiana University Center for Economic Policy Research Discussion Paper 752.

Friedlander, Ann F. 1973. "Macro Policy Goals in the Postwar Period: A Study in Revealed Preferences." *Quarterly Journal of Economics* 87:25–43.

Friedman, Milton. 1953. "The Methodology of Positive Economics." In *Essays in Positive Economics.* Chicago: University of Chicago Press.

Froyen, Richard T., Thomas Havrilesky, and Roger N. Waud. 1997. "The Asymmetric Effects of Political Pressures on U.S. Monetary Policy." *Journal of Macroeconomics* 19 (3): 471–90.

Fuller, William A. 1976. *Introduction to Statistical Time Series.* New York: Wiley.

Gildea, John. 1990. "FOMC Dissent Voting." In *The Political Economy of American Monetary Policy,* edited by Thomas D. Willett. Cambridge: Cambridge University Press.

Goodfriend, Marvin. 1991. "Bureau Analysis and Central Banking: A Review Essay." *Journal of Monetary Economics* 22:517–22.

Granger, C. W. J., and P. Newbold. 1986. *Forecasting Economic Time Series.* 2d ed. Orlando, FL: Academic Press.

Greenwald, John. 1996. "No Room at the Fed." *Time,* 26 February, 57.

Greider, William. 1987. *Secrets of the Temple: How the Federal Reserve Runs the Country.* New York: Simon and Schuster.

Grier, Kevin B. 1986. "Monetary Policy as Political Equilibrium." *Cato Journal* 6:539–43.

Grier, Kevin B. 1987. "Presidential Elections and Federal Reserve Policy: An Empirical Test." *Southern Economic Journal* 54:475–86.

Grier, Kevin B. 1989. "On the Existence of a Political Monetary Cycle." *American Journal of Political Science* 33:376–89.

Grier, Kevin B. 1991. "Congressional Influence on U.S. Monetary Policy." *Journal of Monetary Economics* 28:201–20.

Grier, Kevin B. 1996. "Congressional Oversight Committee Influence on U.S. Monetary Policy Revisited." *Journal of Monetary Economics* 38:571–79.

Grilli, Vittorio, Donato Masciandaro, and Guido Tabellini. 1991. "Political and Monetary Institutions and Public Finance Policies in the Industrial Countries." *Economic Policy* 13:341–92.

Hakes, David R. 1990. "The Objectives and Priorities of Monetary Policy under Different Federal Reserve Chairmen." *Journal of Money, Credit, and Banking* 22:327–37.

Hammond, Thomas H., and Jeffrey S. Hill. 1993. "Deference or Preference? Explaining Senate Confirmation of Presidential Nominees to Administrative Agencies." *Journal of Theoretical Politics* 5 (1): 23–59.

Hammond, Thomas H., and Jack H. Knott. 1996. "Who Controls the Bureaucracy? Presidential Power, Congressional Dominance, Legal Constraints, and Bureaucratic Autonomy in a Model of Multi-Institutional Policymaking." *Journal of Law, Economics, and Organization* 12 (1): 121–68.

Havrilesky, Thomas. 1967. "A Test of Monetary Policy Action." *Journal of Political Economy* 75:299–304.

Havrilesky, Thomas. 1987. "A Partisanship Theory of Monetary and Fiscal Policy Regimes." *Journal of Money, Credit, and Banking* 19:308–25.

Havrilesky, Thomas. 1988. "Monetary Policy Signaling from the Administration to the Federal Reserve." *Journal of Money, Credit, and Banking* 20:83–101.

Havrilesky, Thomas. 1991. "The Federal Reserve Chairman as Hero: Our Defense against Monetary Excesses." *Cato Journal* 13:65–72.

Havrilesky, Thomas. 1994. "Outside Influences on Monetary Policy: A Summary of Recent Findings." *Contemporary Economic Policy* 12:46–51.

Havrilesky, Thomas. 1995. *The Pressures on American Monetary Policy.* 2d ed. Boston: Kluwer.

Havrilesky, Thomas, and John Gildea. 1990. "Packing the Board of Governors." *Challenge* 33 (March–April): 52–55.

Havrilesky, Thomas, and John Gildea. 1991. "The Policy Preferences of FOMC Members as Revealed by Dissenting Votes: A Comment." *Journal of Money, Credit, and Banking* 23:130–38.

Havrilesky, Thomas, and John Gildea. 1992. "Reliable and Unreliable Partisan Appointees to the Board of Governors." *Public Choice* 73:397–417.

Havrilesky, Thomas, and John Gildea. 1995. "The Biases of Federal Reserve Bank Presidents." *Economic Inquiry* 33:274–84.

Haynes, Stephen E., and Joe A. Stone. 1989. "Political Models of the Business Cycle Should be Revived." *Economic Inquiry* 28:442–65.

Herrera, Richard, Thomas Epperlein, and Eric R. A. N. Smith. 1995. "The Stability of Congressional Roll-Call Indexes." *Political Research Quarterly* 48:403–16.

Hetzel, Robert L. 1990. "The Political Economy of Monetary Policy." In *The Political Economy of American Monetary Policy,* edited by Thomas D. Willett. Cambridge: Cambridge University Press.

Hibbs, Douglas. 1977. "Political Parties and Macroeconomic Policy." *American Political Science Review* 71:1467–87.

Hibbs, Douglas. 1987. *The American Political Economy: Electoral Policy and Macroeconomics in Contemporary America.* Cambridge: Harvard University Press.

Hibbs, Douglas. 1994. "The Partisan Model of Macroeconomic Cycles: More Theory and Evidence for the United States." *Economics and Politics* 6:1–24.

Hill, Larry B. 1995. Review of *Bureaucratic Dynamics: The Role of Bureaucracy in a Democracy,* by B. Dan Wood and Richard W. Waterman. *American Political Science Review* 89:770–71.

Hinich, Melvin J., and Michael C. Munger. 1997. *Analytical Politics.* Cambridge: Cambridge University Press.

House Hearings on the Conduct of Monetary Policy. 1976, 1977, 1978. Washington, DC: Government Printing Office.

Huxtable, Philip A. 1994. "Incorporating the Rules Committee: An Extension of the Ferejohn/Shipan Model." *Journal of Law, Economics, and Organization* 10:160–67.

Kane, Edward J. 1980. "Politics and Fed Policymaking: The More Things Change the More They Stay the Same." *Journal of Monetary Economics* 17:199–212.

Kane, Edward J. 1982. "External Pressure and the Operations of the Fed." In *The Political Economy of International and Domestic Monetary Policy,* edited by Raymond E. Lombra and Willard E. Witte. Ames: Iowa State University Press.

Kane, Edward J. 1988. "The Impact of a New Federal Reserve Chairman." *Contemporary Policy Issues* 6:10–16.

Kane, Edward J. 1990. "Bureaucratic Self-Interest as an Obstacle to Monetary Reform." In *The Political Economy of American Monetary Policy,* edited by Thomas A. Mayer. Cambridge: Cambridge University Press.

Keech, William R. 1995. *Economic Politics: The Cost of Democracy.* Cambridge: Cambridge University Press.

Keech, William R., and Irwin Morris. 1995. "Central Bank Independence as a Choice Variable: The Case of the 1951 Fed-Treasury Accord." Paper presented at the annual meeting of the Public Choice Society, Long Beach, CA.

Keech, William R., and Irwin Morris. 1997. "Appointments, Presidential Power, and the Federal Reserve." *Journal of Macroeconomics* 19 (2): 253–67.

Kettl, Donald F. 1986. *Leadership at the Fed.* New Haven: Yale University Press.

Khoury, Salwa S. 1990 "Reaction Functions." In *The Political Economy of American Monetary Policy,* edited by Thomas A. Mayer. Cambridge: Cambridge University Press.

Kiewiet, Roderick, and Matthew McCubbins. 1991. *The Logic of Congressional Action.* Chicago: University of Chicago Press.

King, Gary, Robert O. Keohane, and Sidney Verba. 1994. *Designing Social Inquiry: Scientific Inference in Qualitative Research.* Princeton: Princeton University Press.

Kmenta, J. 1986. *Elements of Econometrics.* New York: Macmillan.

Knott, Jack H. 1984. "Protective Organizational Strategies of the Federal Reserve Board." Paper presented at the annual meeting of the Midwest Political Science Association, Chicago.

Knott, Jack H., and Gary J. Miller. 1987. *Reforming Bureaucracy: The Politics of Institutional Choice.* Englewood Cliffs, NJ: Prentice-Hall.

Krause, George. 1994. "Federal Reserve Policy Decision Making: Political and Bureaucratic Influences." *American Journal of Political Science* 38:124–44.

Krause, George, and Jim Granato. 1996. "Rational Expectations within the Electorate: Formal Tests with Heterogeneous Agents." Paper presented at the annual meeting of the Midwest Political Science Association, Chicago.

Krehbiel, Keith. 1994. "Deference, Extremism, and Interest Group Ratings." *Legislative Studies Quarterly* 19:61–77.

LeRoy, Stephen F. 1984. "Nominal Prices and Interest Rates in General Equilibrium: Money Shocks." *Journal of Business* 57 (April): 177–95.

Levi, Maurice D., and John H. Makin. 1978. "Anticipated Inflation and Interest Rates: Further Interpretation of Findings on the Fisher Equation." *American Economic Review* 68 (December): 801–12.

Lucas, Robert E., Jr. 1973. "Some International Evidence on Output-Inflation Tradeoffs." *American Economic Review* 63:326–35.

Lupia, Arthur, and Matthew D. McCubbins. 1994. "Learning from Oversight: Fire Alarms and Police Patrols Reconstructed." *Journal of Law, Economics, and Organization* 10:96–125.

Mayer, Thomas. 1990. "Minimizing Regret: Cognitive Dissonance as an Explanation of FOMC Behavior." In *The Political Economy of American Monetary Policy,* edited by Thomas D. Willett. Cambridge: Cambridge University Press.

McCubbins, Matthew D. 1985 "The Legislative Design of Regulatory Structure." *American Journal of Political Science* 29:721–48.

McCubbins, Matthew D., and Thomas Schwartz. 1984. "Congressional Oversight Overlooked: Police Patrols versus Fire Alarms." *American Journal of Political Science* 28:165–79.

McNees, Stephen K. 1986. "Modeling the Fed: A Forward-Looking Monetary

Policy Reaction Function." *New England Economic Review* (November–December): 3–8.

Miller, Gary J., and Terry Moe. 1983. "Bureaucrats, Legislators, and Size of Government.'" *American Political Science Review* 77:297–322.

Mills, T. C. 1990. *Time Series Techniques for Economists.* Cambridge: Cambridge University Press.

Moe, Terry. 1982. "Regulatory Performance and Presidential Administrations.'" *American Journal of Political Science* 26:197–224.

Moe, Terry. 1984. "The New Economics of Organization.'" *American Journal of Political Science* 28:739–77.

Moe, Terry. 1985. "Control and Feedback in Economic Regulation: The Case of the NLRB." *American Political Science Review* 79:1094–16.

Moe, Terry. 1987. "Congressional Control of the Bureaucracy: An Assessment of the Positive Theory of 'Congressional Dominance.'" *Legislative Studies Quarterly* 12:475–520.

Morris, Irwin. 1995. "Monetary Policy Signaling and the Senate Banking Committee." *Social Science Quarterly* 76:902–10.

Morris, Irwin, and Michael Munger. 1998. "First Branch or Root: The Congress, the President, and the Federal Reserve." *Public Choice* 96:363–80.

Munger, Michael C., and Brian E. Roberts. 1990. "The Federal Reserve and Its Institutional Environment: A Review." In *The Political Economy of American Monetary Policy,* edited by Thomas D. Willett. Cambridge: Cambridge University Press.

Nathan, Richard. 1983. *The Administrative Presidency.* New York: Wiley.

Neuman, Manfred. 1991. "Precommitment by Central Bank Independence." *Open Economies Review* 2:95–112.

Newton, Maxwell. 1983. *The Fed: Inside the Federal Reserve, the Secret Power Center That Controls the American Economy.* New York: Times Books.

Niskanen, William. 1971. *Bureaucracy and Representative Government.* Chicago: Aldine-Atherton.

Noll, Roger G. 1971. *Reforming Regulation.* Washington, DC: Brookings Institution.

Ogul, Morris S. 1976. *Congress Oversees the Bureaucracy: Studies in Legislative Supervision.* Pittsburgh: University of Pittsburgh Press.

Ogul, Morris S., and Bert A. Rockman. 1990. "Overseeing Oversight: New Departures and Old Problems." *Legislative Studies Quarterly* 15:5–24.

Pious, Richard. 1979. *The American Presidency.* New York: Basic Books.

Plott, Charles R. 1991. "Will Economics Become an Experimental Science?" *Southern Economic Journal* 57:901–20.

Posen, Adam S. 1993. "Why Central Bank Independence Does Not Cause Low Inflation: There Is No Institutional Fix for Politics." In *Finance and the International Economy,* vol. 7, edited by R. O'Brien. Oxford: Oxford University Press.

Quinn, Dennis, and Robert Shapiro. 1991. "Economic Growth Strategies: The

Effects of Ideological Partisanship on Interest Rates and Business Taxation in the United States." *American Journal of Political Science* 35:656–85.

Reuber, G. L. 1964. "The Objectives of Canadian Monetary Policy, 1949–1961: Empirical 'Trade-Offs' and the Reaction Function of the Authorities." *Journal of Political Economy* 72:109–32.

Riker, William H. 1980. "Implications from the Disequilibrium of Majority Rule for the Study of Institutions." *American Political Science Review* 74:432–46.

Riker, William H. 1982. *Liberalism against Populism: A Confrontation between the Theory of Democracy and the Theory of Social Choice.* San Francisco: Freeman.

Ringquist, Evan J. 1995. "Political Control and Policy Impact in EPA's Office of Water Quality." *American Journal of Political Science* 39 (2): 336–63.

Rockman, Bert A. 1984. "Legislative-Executive Relations and Legislative Oversight." *Legislative Studies Quarterly* 9:387–440.

Rogoff, Kenneth. 1990. "Equilibrium Political Business Cycles." *American Economic Review* 80:21–36.

Rogoff, Kenneth, and Anne Sibert. 1988. "Elections and Macroeconomic Policy Cycles." *Review of Economic Studies* 55:1–16.

Rose, Sanford. 1974. "The Agony of the Federal Reserve." *Fortune,* (July): 91–98.

Scholz, John T., and Feng Heng Wei. 1986. "Regulatory Enforcement in a Federalist System." *American Political Science Review* 80:1249–70.

Senate Hearings on the Conduct of Monetary Policy. 1976, 1977. Washington, DC: Government Printing Office.

Shughart, William F., and Robert D. Tollison. 1986. "Preliminary Evidence on the Use of Inputs by the Federal Reserve System." In *Central Bankers, Bureaucratic Incentives, and Monetary Policy,* edited by Eugenia Toma and Mark Toma. Boston: Kluwer.

Shull, Bernard. 1995–96. "Federal Reserve Independence: What Kind and How Much?" *Journal of Post-Keynesian Economics* 18:211–30.

Snyder, James M. 1992. "Artificial Extremism in Interest Group Ratings." *Legislative Studies Quarterly* 17:319–45.

Spitzer, Matthew. 1990. "Extensions of Ferejohn and Shipan's Model of Administrative Agency Behavior." *Journal of Law, Economics, and Organization* 6 (spring): 29–43.

Steunenberg, Bernard. 1992. "Congress, Bureaucracy, and Regulatory Policy-Making." *Journal of Law, Economics, and Organization* 8:673–94.

Steunenberg, Bernard. 1996. "Agent Discretion, Regulatory Policymaking, and Different Institutional Arrangements." *Public Choice* 86:309–39.

Taylor, John B. 1980. "Aggregate Dynamics and Staggered Contracts." *Journal of Political Economy* 88:1–23.

Timberlake, Richard H. 1993. *Monetary Policy in the United States.* Chicago: University of Chicago Press.

Toma, Mark. 1982. "Inflationary Bias of the Federal Reserve System: A Bureaucratic Perspective." *Journal of Monetary Economics* 10:163–90.

Toma, Mark. 1991. "The Demise of the Public-Interest Model of the Federal Reserve System." *Journal of Monetary Economics* 27:157–63.

Toma, Eugenia, and Mark Toma. 1986. *Central Bankers, Bureaucratic Incentives, and Monetary Policy.* Boston: Kluwer.

Tufte, Edward R. 1978. *Political Control of the Economy.* Princeton: Princeton University Press.

Van Damme, Eric. 1987. *Stability and Perfection of Nash Equilibria.* Berlin: Springer-Verlag.

Vandoren, Peter M. 1990. "Can We Learn the Causes of Congressional Decisions from Roll-Call Data?" *Legislative Studies Quarterly* 15:311–40.

Waller, Christopher J. 1992. "A Bargaining Model of Partisan Appointments to the Central Bank." *Journal of Monetary Economics* 29:411–28.

Waller, Christopher J., and Carl E. Walsh. 1994. "Central Bank Independence, Economic Behavior, and Optimal Term Lengths." Unpublished ms.

Waterman, Richard W. 1989. *Presidential Influence and the Administrative State.* Knoxville: University of Tennessee Press.

Weingast, Barry. 1981. "Regulation, Reregulation, and Deregulation: The Political Foundations of Agency-Clientele Relationships." *Law and Contemporary Problems* 44:147–77.

Weingast, Barry. 1984. "The Congressional-Bureaucratic System: A Principal-Agent Perspective." *Public Choice* 44:147–91.

Weingast, Barry, and William Marshall. 1988. "The Industrial Organization of Congress." *Journal of Political Economy* 96:132–63.

Weingast, Barry, and Mark Moran. 1982. "The Myth of Runaway Bureaucracy: The Case of the FTC." *Regulation* 6:33–38.

Weingast, Barry, and Mark Moran. 1983. "Bureaucratic Discretion or Congressional Oversight? Regulatory Policy-Making by the Federal Trade Commission." *Journal of Political Economy* 91:765–800.

Weintraub, Robert E. 1978. "Congressional Supervision of Monetary Policy." *Journal of Monetary Economics* 4:341–62.

Wicker, Elmus. 1993. "The U.S. Central Banking Experience: A Historical Perspective." In *Handbook of Comparative Economic Policies,* Vol. 3., *Monetary Policy in Developed Economies,* edited by Michele U. Fratianni and Dominick Salvatore. Westport, CT: Greenwood.

Williams, John. 1990. "The Political Manipulation of Macroeconomic Policy." *American Political Science Review* 84:767–95.

Wilson, James Q. 1980. *The Politics of Regulation.* New York: Basic Books.

Wilson, James Q. 1989. *Bureaucracy: What Government Agencies Do and Why They Do It.* New York: Basic Books.

Wood, B. Dan. 1988. "Principals, Bureaucrats, and Responsiveness in Clean Air Enforcements." *American Political Science Review* 82:213–34.

Wood, B. Dan, and James Anderson. 1993. "The Politics of U.S. Antitrust Regulation." *American Journal of Political Science* 37:1–39.

Wood, B. Dan, and Richard W. Waterman. 1991. "The Dynamics of Political Control of the Bureaucracy." *American Political Science Review* 85:801–28.

Wood, B. Dan, and Richard W. Waterman. 1993. "The Dynamics of Political-Bureaucratic Adaptation." *American Journal of Political Science* 37:497–528.

Wood, B. Dan, and Richard W. Waterman. 1994. *Bureaucratic Dynamics: The Role of Bureaucracy in a Democracy.* Boulder, CO: Westview.

Wood, John H. 1967. "A Model of Federal Reserve Behavior." In *Monetary Process and Policy: A Symposium,* edited by George Horwich. Homewood, IL: Irwin.

Woolley, John T. 1984. *The Federal Reserve and the Politics of Monetary Policy.* Cambridge: Cambridge University Press.

Woolley, John T. 1988. "Partisan Manipulation of the Economy: Another Look at Monetary Policy with Moving Regression." *Journal of Politics* 50:335–60.

Woolley, John T. 1993. "Conflict among Regulators and the Hypothesis of Congressional Dominance." *Journal of Politics* 55:92–114.

Woolley, John T. 1994. "The Politics of Monetary Policy: A Critical Review." *Journal of Public Policy* 14:57–85.

Yohe, William P. 1966. "A Study of Federal Open Market Committee Voting." *Southern Economic Journal* 12:396–405.

Young, Kelly. 1997. "Their People = Their Policy: The President, Congress, and Appointments to the Federal Reserve." Paper presented at the annual meeting of the Midwest Political Science Association, Chicago.

Index